Facilitator Notes

for

Getting Ahead in a Just-Gettin'-By World

Building Your Resources for a Better Life

DeVol, Philip E.
    Facilitator Notes for Getting Ahead in a Just-Gettin'-By World:
        Building Your Resources for a Better Life (Revised Edition, 2006). 87 pp.
    Bibliography pp. 85–87
    ISBN 10: 1-929229-36-4
    ISBN 13: 978-1-929229-36-9

1. Education   2. Sociology   3. Conduct of life   4. Title

Copy editing by Dan Shenk

OTHER TITLES

Getting Ahead in a Just-Gettin'-By World: Building Your Resources for a Better Life
    Philip E. DeVol

Bridges Out of Poverty: Strategies for Professionals and Communities
    Ruby K. Payne, Ph.D., Philip DeVol, Terie Dreussi Smith

A Framework for Understanding Poverty
    Ruby K. Payne, Ph.D.

FACILITATOR NOTES

for

Getting Ahead in a Just-Gettin'-By World

Building Your Resources for a Better Life

Philip E. DeVol

TABLE OF CONTENTS

PHILOSOPHY

Thank you for taking on the important work of sharing the concepts of Dr. Ruby K. Payne with people in poverty. Being an early adopter—and adapter—of Ruby Payne's work is both a privilege and a challenge. It's a privilege to work on such an important issue, and it's a challenge because moving from poverty to prosperity is very hard to do. We will be working both with people in poverty and people in the community to make the transition possible.

This work can be a transforming experience for you, as well as the participants. If you choose to relax your professional boundaries a little you'll find that this will be a learning experience for you too. Also, the topics of poverty, prosperity, and community sustainability are so compelling that you will likely be challenged to expand your exploration of the topics and add to your reading list. This is not a scripted curriculum; it requires additional and deeper learning on the part of the facilitator.

Theory of Change

If we agree on the theory of change that underlies this work it will allow us to be flexible and consistent in the way we present the information.

We will be sharing the theory of change with the participants, henceforth referred to as investigators, so they will understand what we are trying to do and so they can monitor their own progress as we move through the workbook.

Theories of change are often very involved and complex. In a way, ours is too, but it helps to state the case in as few words as possible, to boil it down to its essential ideas. Our theory starts with the way we understand the problem.

Poverty traps people in the tyranny of the moment, making it very difficult to attend to abstract information or plan for the future—the very things needed to build adequate resources and financial assets. There are many causes of poverty, some having to do with the choices of the poor, but most stemming from community conditions and political/economic structures. The theory of change must take all of this into account.

Our theory of change

People in poverty need an accurate perception of how poverty impacts them and an understanding of economic realities as a starting point both for reasoning and for developing plans for transition. Using mental models for comprehension and reasoning, people can move from the concrete to the abstract. Using Payne's definition of the resources necessary for a full life and her insights into the hidden rules of economic class, people can evaluate themselves, choose behaviors, and make plans to build resources and climb out of poverty. The community must provide services, support, and meaningful opportunities over the long term. In partnership with people from middle class and wealth, individuals in poverty can solve community **and** *systemic problems that contribute to poverty.*

Getting Ahead in a Just-Gettin'-By World is designed to facilitate this theory of change. What follows is an expanded explanation of the theory. What appears in the *Getting Ahead* workbook is in **bold-face** type.

- **Living in poverty makes it hard for people to change. The "What It's Like Now" experience is a trap that forces people to live in the moment and, in many cases, in chaos.**

  Premise: The poor are trapped in the tyranny of survival, which demands concrete solutions and makes it difficult to attend to abstract concepts (Payne, Freire, Feuerstein, Galeano).

- **Because of this, it is especially important that people in poverty come to understand the big picture of poverty, to learn that poverty is about more than the choices they make.**

  Premise: The research identifies many causes of poverty; therefore there must be a wide array of strategies to reduce poverty (O'Connor, Brouwer, Gans).

  Premise: The process of change is enhanced if the person can separate the problem from himself/herself (Freedman, Combs).

- **It also is important to learn how poverty impacts individuals. So ... learning about the hidden rules of economic class, resources, family structure, and language issues is crucial to doing a critical analysis of the situation.**

  Premise: Payne's hidden rules of economic class are a unique analytic category regarding economic issues; more typical categories are race and gender. The hidden rules can be used for understanding, describing, analyzing, and predicting behavior (Payne).

- **When people in poverty understand the big picture, as well as their own issues, they will know what to do.**

  Premise: People in poverty can be trusted to make good use of accurate information, presented in a meaningful way by facilitators who provide a relationship of mutual respect and act as co-investigators (Johnson-Laird, Freire, Sapolsky, McKnight, Pransky, Farson).

  Premise: Individuals must generate their own motivation and plans for change (Miller).

Premise: Mental models can be used to help people living in poverty move from the concrete to the abstract to find new, yet concrete, solutions (Freire, Johnson-Laird, Harrison, Payne).

Premise: Mental models help people learn quickly and without over-reliance on language (Payne, Freire, Feuerstein, Sapolsky, Mattaini).

- **Doing a self-assessment of personal resources and an assessment of community resources will allow individuals to make their own plans for economic stability.**

Premise: Ultimately, the work of assessing and planning for all aspects of one's life lies with the individual (Freire, Andreas, Faulkner; Freedman, Combs; Miller, Rollnick).

- **Using the hidden rules of economic class to build resources will ease the transition to stability.**

Premise: If people in poverty use Payne's definitions of hidden rules and resources, they will be able to more accurately assess their own internal and external assets (Payne, Krabill).

- **Partnerships with the middle class and other people will build crucial social support.**

Premise: No matter the economic class, people strive to earn the respect of their peers. A bridge of enhanced social capital is needed by which a person can earn respect in new places, with new people (Fussell, Putnam).

Premise: Individuals who are in the process of developing their own economic security need support to stabilize situations during transitions (Payne).

- **Working on individual plans is not enough because poverty is a systems problem too. Plans must be made to address community problems.**

Premise: A partnership among all three economic classes is needed to bring about economic stability (Phillips).

Premise: Mental models are necessary for the development of effective community strategies to build prosperity (Jaworski, Harrison, Senge).

- **People in poverty are problem solvers.**

  Premise: An accurate mental model of people in poverty is that they are community problem solvers as opposed to the prevailing perception that defines the poor as needy and deficient (McKnight, Pransky, Henderson).

Process of Change

- *Sequence and reinforcement*: *Getting Ahead* is presented in a particular sequence. It follows the pathway laid out by the first few groups to investigate poverty using this approach. It is important to follow the sequence and to reinforce the learning as you move along. Jane Vella, author of *Learning to Listen, Learning to Teach*, says, "When we work diligently to design learning tasks that are in simple and sound sequence and that reinforce learning, we address the disparity in political power more directly than if we preach loudly on social and economic injustice. These rather technical principles and practices—reinforcement and sequence—are tough to use. They demand attention and diligence to design. When you do that hard work, you are in fact addressing sociopolitical-economic inequalities. It is all of a piece."

- *The process:* The triangle introduced in Module 1 describes how this theory of change is presented. In a nutshell it works like this:

  Learn about poverty in the broad sense.
  Learn Ruby Payne's framework.
  Learn how poverty impacts you.
  Assess your own resources.
  Assess community resources.
  Think about it; analyze it.
  Make your plans for building resources.
  Monitor your motivation and your changes throughout.

- *Trust the process:* The first time you take a group through the workbook you are going to wonder if it's working. Questioning the process, along with feeling the urge to fix things, are natural. Resist the urge to react to all the things that worry you. After you've gone through the workbook a couple of times, you'll trust the process and let many things sort themselves out. Here are some thoughts to keep in mind:

  This is a "kitchen table" learning experience for adults who are investigating new information in the context of their lives. It does not resemble in any way the typical classroom environment. There is no lecturing, no PowerPoint presentation, and no one standing at the head of the class.

  People who go through this experience with you are to be referred to as investigators. Investigators are active; they question, they look into things, dig for facts, look for patterns, analyze the data, and find answers. These investigators will be examining their own lives and the conditions in their communities. Eventually they will be answerable to themselves, and it is anticipated that they will become problem solvers in their own community context.

This isn't group therapy, so it isn't your job to resolve longstanding emotional issues or even conflicts that people may have.

Some members of the group will have been in therapeutic groups, which can be helpful or unhelpful. On the positive side, they may have learned the responsibilities of group membership. On the negative side, they may need to be reminded of the nature and scope of this group and its rules.

Clarifying the group rules in the first session (see "Making It Safe and Challenging" on page 5) will go a long way toward preventing most problems. It's a good idea to review them from time to time.

Some members of the group will use the participatory discourse pattern and circular story pattern. When people arrive for the sessions (and sometimes even in the middle of the session) general talking or side conversations will likely break out. Most of these conversations have to do with survival; they're about a recent crisis, a relationship, or the sharing of survival tips. It's unlikely that any of these are about the abstract information contained in the workbook. It would be a mistake to treat this in a heavy-handed way when it's really an opportunity to learn. Don't miss the chance to learn something that might help you or the group—some nuance of predatory lending, for example, or an illustration of how a hidden rule was broken. Take a few minutes (no more than 5–8) for individuals to share with the larger group what you were overhearing. Write these things down on chart paper. Once these insights are listed, you can move on more quickly the next time the topic comes up. Anytime after the theory of change has been introduced, these conversations can be described as conversations about the "concrete." The more time spent talking about being stuck, the less time we have to talk about getting unstuck. *NOTE:* It also will be affirming to the individuals who share in this way that the "stuff" they bring naturally can and will be useful to the larger group.

Groups tend to act in predictable ways. The phases of most groups include:

1) *Kissing up*—Everyone tries hard to earn the respect of the leader and be helpful.
2) *Storming*—The rules are tested, and people assert their independence.
3) *Norming*—Patterns, rules, and unspoken rules are established and adhered to.
4) *Performing*—The members work hard, building on each other's ideas; people begin to appreciate each other.

All this can happen in a jury room, for example, as 12 strangers come together and start deliberating. Watch for these phases, keep notes on the process, and you'll likely see this unfold.

Participation in a group can be enhanced by the facilitator using the following kinds of strategies:

1) Do a "round robin" at the beginning of each session, asking each person to answer a question. Some examples are … "What is one thing you remember from the last session? Is there anything going on with you that might make it difficult to pay attention today?" It's a good idea to establish a time limit on the answers! This gives everyone a chance to say something, to establish that he/she is "present" today.
2) If someone is holding back, ask him/her what's up.
3) Have people show "thumbs." Thumbs up, agree; thumbs down, disagree; thumbs to the side, neutral.
4) Break the group into sets of two or three people and have them discuss a point and report back to the group.
5) Ask for volunteers to assist you by writing on chart paper.
6) When you start doing mental models, have people share theirs. The idea behind mental models is to use one another's thinking to build better models. Finally, don't forget that even the quiet group members are probably learning. If someone just doesn't want to verbalize, allow him/her to "pass."

- *Concrete to abstract to concrete:* People in poverty live in the concrete but, if they're going to make changes, they need to be in the abstract where they can get new ideas. So … we offer the abstract in the form of research on the causes of poverty, Ruby Payne's framework, and information on how change takes place. Most people in poverty can't use the abstract unless it's made concrete and relevant. Because of this, we offer the concrete in the form of mental models, assessments, worksheets, and detailed planning steps.

- *Critical analysis:* We trust that people can and will do an accurate analysis of the information and their situation—and that they'll know what needs to be done.

- *The stages of change:* The stages introduced in Module 7 are: pre-contemplation, contemplation, preparation, action, and maintenance. This workbook is designed to take individuals up to and through the "preparation" stage. The "action" stage takes place when they leave the group, plan in hand. Maintenance, of course, comes even later. This workbook is about understanding, motivation, and empowerment. It gives people a vision and a taste of things to come.

- *Listening precedes dialogue, dialogue precedes action:* We begin by listening, by reversing the flow of information. Listening bridges distrust and builds relationships. We don't leap to obvious conclusions or give people "the" solutions. People in poverty get enough of that from the agencies. Action—knowing what to do—arises out of the meaning of the dialogue.

- *Timeline:* All of this is to occur in 15 sessions of 2½ hours each! The facilitator's greatest challenge is getting everything done in 15 sessions.

Motivation

Our goal is for the investigators, not us, to make the argument for change. Our process is designed to promote motivation by creating a discrepancy between life as it is now and what it might be in the future. The "What It's Like Now" mental model created in Module 2 is the baseline for that discrepancy-making process. It names, describes, and analyzes the impact of poverty on the investigator. We must not allow ourselves to make the argument for change. Resist the urge!

The role of the facilitator is described best by William Miller and Stephen Rollnick in *Motivational Interviewing: Preparing People for Change.*

> Carl Rogers articulated and tested a theory about critical counselor skills for facilitating change. He asserted that a client-centered interpersonal relationship—in which the counselor manifests three critical conditions— provides the ideal atmosphere for change to occur. Within the context of such a safe and supportive atmosphere, clients are free to explore their experiences openly and to reach resolutions of their own problems. The counselor's role, in Rogers' view, is not a directive one of providing solutions, suggestions, or analysis. Instead, the counselor need only offer these three critical conditions to prepare the way for natural change: accurate empathy, non-possessive warmth, and genuineness.

One of the unique features of our approach is that we pay people to participate in problem solving. This requires a rationale. But first, let's distinguish between motivation for change and an incentive to attend a workgroup. An incentive may get someone to attend a workgroup for 15 sessions; it is *not* sufficient to generate motivation to make life changes.

On the other hand, an individual is not likely to make life changes without getting new information that can only be obtained by attending.

Rationale for the incentive or payment

It's important to explain our reasoning for offering an incentive because a payment conflicts with the middle-class sensibility that says you shouldn't have to be paid to learn something that is going to better your life. Case in point: Middle-class students and their families pay for college, not the other way around.

People who live in poverty are living in the concrete or, as Paulo Freire puts it, the tyranny of the moment. The problems the investigators face require immediate action and, when a person must *act*, he/she will not be willing or able to learn. The security of a middle-class income allows people to know that today's needs are met so they can afford to focus on the future and the abstract.

Folks who live in the concrete can motivate themselves to move toward something or away from something. In either case, though, it's an immediate reaction. So asking people from poverty to participate in a program that has some possible distant reward isn't going to work any more than the "thou shalts" of the middle class have worked.

This workbook is about change, and change is difficult for people in poverty. Richard Farson, author of *Management of the Absurd*, says that individuals with the most resources find it easiest to change; those with the least find it hardest. Incidentally, this is true of organizations too.

Paradoxically, for people to change (get sober, climb out of poverty, build assets) they have to move from the concrete to the abstract. So … helping people move into the abstract becomes a key issue.

People who run such programs have found that incentives are needed to get people to attend. Once a relationship is established, people may attend partly because of the relationship, because they like the instructor. When the value of the information is realized, however, that may become the greatest incentive.

Incentives are to be framed as payment for something that must be done, something beyond attendance. The investigator gets paid after each session, but that's only the "pay period." The work the investigators do is to create an assessment of the community and develop mental models for prosperity for themselves and the community. This sets up the expectation that investigators are to produce something and underscores the fact that they are problem solvers.

Finally, if the organization doesn't typically provide incentives for investigators, it may take a little creative thinking on the part of administrators and fiscal officers to get this done.

Facilitator Role as Someone from Dominant Culture

Those who have worked on poverty or diversity issues are familiar with the quandary of the facilitator's hierarchical position. There is no escaping two conflicting and co-existing realities. One is the distrust that people in poverty have for authority and agencies. This can be ameliorated, but *only somewhat*, if the facilitator is from poverty, because he/she is an employee of an agency, and/or he/she may be a member of some other group that disqualifies him/her from automatic credibility. The second reality is that people with more resources and a broader perspective have something of value to offer those who are trapped in the moment.

Freire's *Pedagogy of the Oppressed* contains the deepest exploration of this dilemma and the best guide for an educator or instructor. Dean Lobovits and John Prowell, writing about narrative approaches, offer guidance to the facilitator in their article "Unexpected Journey: Invitations to Diversity."

Key concepts

Poverty in the United States is a complex, multi-layered problem that can be approached from many angles; race, ethnicity, gender, age, religion, sexual orientation, politics, and class. In *Getting Ahead* we use economic class as the analytic category while encouraging investigators and the facilitator to explore local cultural-diversity issues that arise.

- *Defining a dominated group:* Members of a dominated group either share a common fate or are perceived by the dominant group to share a common fate. People from a distinct racial, ethnic, or religious group, such as recent immigrants from Cambodia or Africa, are likely to identify themselves with the group and recognize that their fates are linked. On the other hand, some people in poverty, even those of the same race or ethnic background, may not feel that their fates are linked. In other words, the individual *does* feel part of the dominant culture. Yet, it is the dominant culture that perceives him/her as a member of a group with a shared fate—as with poor whites, for example. When going through this workbook, some investigators may for the first time begin to identify themselves as being in poverty and as being part of a group with a shared fate. As facilitators, we need to be aware that this is occurring.

  The implication for facilitators is this: If we don't acknowledge that some people feel dominated or threatened by us, and if we don't have a way of dealing with the dominator/dominated issue, we will fail to establish the relationship that enhances the transfer of information.

  In addition, we as facilitators must be aware that if we aren't careful, we may contribute to the "false generosity" of the dominant culture. False generosity includes paternalistic attitudes and "caring for" strategies that are most easily spotted in the missionary to the "dark continent," but they're just as real in the mindset of many essentially good-hearted politicians and social workers here in the United States.

- *The fate of the middle class:* As facilitators, it would be wise to consider the fate of the middle class. The middle class is declining for the first time since the beginning of the industrial revolution. Well-paying manufacturing jobs have gone overseas and now white-collar, knowledge-sector jobs, are going there too. The divide between the rich and poor occurs at the 10% mark. Ninety percent of us are sliding down as the top 10% are becoming increasingly wealthy. Several writers on economic issues suggest that the middle class should wake up; its fate is linked to that of the poor. The question becomes: Is this trend sustainable?

- *Education that transforms:* In the foreword to *Pedagogy of the Oppressed,* Richard Shaull writes:

  > There is no such thing as a *neutral* educational process. Education either functions as an instrument that is used to facilitate the integrations of the younger generation into the logic of the present system and bring about conformity to it, *or* it

becomes "the practice of freedom," the means by which men and women deal critically and creatively with reality and discover how to participate in the transformation of their world.

One reason typical efforts to educate people in generational poverty have not worked is that they failed to challenge people to "deal critically and creatively with reality." Instead, they went straight to teaching the logic of the present system with classes in literacy, financial knowledge, job-seeking skills, workplace skills, and the like. This workbook is unique in that it deals with the realities of a political/economic system that contributes to poverty and trusts the investigators to analyze their situation, to solve problems, and to transform their world.

- _Two story lines:_ Facilitators will be working with two story lines throughout this workbook. One is the collective story of all people in poverty, starting with the creation of a mental model for poverty, then moving through the hidden rules of class and language experience. The second story line applies to individuals: their history, the impact that poverty has had on them, and the degree to which they do without specific resources.

  In both these instances, the role of the facilitator will be to separate the problem from the person. In _Narrative Therapy: The Social Construction of Preferred Realities_, Jill Freedman and Gene Combs suggest that the way the questions are asked can facilitate change. When we ask, "How has poverty affected you?" we help create intellectual distance or detachment that _facilitates change_. This is different from laying the blame for a person's circumstances on him/her directly as if poverty had everything to do with the choices of the poor and nothing to do with larger community and national factors. Framing the questions in this way means that group members don't have to defend themselves.

- _Raising the difficult issues:_ As representatives of the dominant culture, facilitators need to be the ones to raise the issues that usually fall to the people in the dominated group: racism, predators, injustices, unfair banking practices, and so on. When those who are dominated raise these issues, it forces them into the role of complainer or radical—and may even suggest that they are speaking for the dominated group. Being forced into one of those roles takes away from any other role they might play: mediator, creative thinker, or leader. When the _facilitator_ raises a controversial issue, the people from the dominated group are free to respond in any number of ways. In this workbook, the facilitator is the one who shares the details and historical trends of inadequate housing, low-wage jobs, and predators. The partnership between the facilitator and co-facilitator, who can act as a "bridging" person, can serve as an avenue for exploring the information and evaluating the relationship between the facilitator and the group.

- _Choice, power, and accountability:_ The main theme of our work is for investigators to analyze their own situations, assess their own resources, and choose their own plans of action. Facilitators will share the hidden rules of class and assist investigators to acquire the power they need to meet their goals. Power can take any number of forms, starting with power over oneself, as well as over one's own thinking and emotions. Then there is the power of language and negotiation and, finally, the power of connections and political/economic influence.

Linked to power and choice is responsibility … the responsibility for the outcomes and the actions that are taken. People who live reactive lives and have little opportunity to make significant choices—people who have little power or influence—are not likely to feel responsible for whatever occurs, for the outcomes. On the other hand, people who have practiced making choices and using power throughout their lives are more likely to be accountable to themselves and others.

"Accountability" is sweeping the land. Fourth-graders and their teachers are held accountable; people who seek work and their caseworkers are held accountable; addicts and their counselors are held accountable. Accountability in its politicized form is greatly debated, clumsily done, and unevenly administered. For people in poverty, accountability is just another name for punishment; it's just one more time the middle class "lays down the law."

And yet, accountability is a positive attribute when it arises from within the person as a result of his/her use of choice and power. Facilitators need to hold to this form of accountability; it is a far better model than the "caring for" model, which fosters manipulation and dependency.

Our form of accountability has these characteristics:

- o All information is presented in a way that is relevant, including information about accountability. For people in poverty, it has to apply to the concrete situation. This is one reason we hire co-facilitators from previous classes; they know how to make information more relevant.
- o Expectations must be communicated clearly, concretely, and respectfully.
- o Ideally, people will be accountable to themselves and others, perhaps even to the *Getting Ahead* group itself.
- o The expectations are related to the systems and structures of the group, agency, community, or nation.
- o People are met where they are. For example, for those who have mental health difficulties, addiction problems, or some sort of disability, the units of accountability are smaller and more immediate.
- o Accountability is framed as choices with natural and logical consequences.
- o Support must be provided for people who are learning to be accountable.
- o When the above conditions are in place, people are held accountable for their choices. A consequence may be that they can't continue with the workgroup.

When any consequences are applied, they are handled face to face, not by letter. In this way mediation can occur, and the relationship can be maintained.

Role of Co-Facilitator(s)

The first time you use the workbook you will be the only facilitator. The second and all subsequent times you will have one or two co-facilitators from the previous group or groups. It is part of our philosophy to use co-facilitators because they:

1) Can make the material relevant.
2) Can help bridge the initial distrust of the group members.
3) Will learn the material more thoroughly by assisting as a co-facilitator.
4) Will be building bridging social capital with you.
5) Can earn respect by assisting you.
6) Can help monitor and help improve the facilitator's performance as a member of the dominant class.

Co-facilitators will be paid to:
1) Participate in the group just as anyone else does, doing the exercises, etc.
2) Model how to explore ideas, how to be a healthy group member.
3) Assist with getting ideas across in informal ways.
4) Assist in evaluating and planning each session and, most importantly, will be required to …
5) Get together with investigators who miss a class to bring them up to speed with the rest of the group so that everyone arrives at the class ready to go—at the same place in the content of the workbook.

Depending on gifts, talents, skills, and interests of the co-facilitators, you may have them present information directly.

Role of Community Agencies and Organizations

The groundwork done in the community prior to conducting a group will determine the experience and success of workgroup members during the action phase, which occurs after they have finished the workbook. Community agencies that share the aha! Process understanding of poverty, as well as the philosophy of this workbook, will be more likely to offer consistent approaches and support for workgroup members. Remember, the goal of this workbook is to help people develop specific goals for enhancing resources. Picture the investigators going to a community agency with their own plans in hand, motivated to utilize the resources offered by that agency. How that agency responds to someone motivated in that way can make a big difference to the person's future.

Recruiting group members

As we begin using this workbook it's important to choose investigators, agencies, and communities carefully. That is to say, we'll want to start where we have a good chance of success, where the conditions favor the investigators. After gaining some experience with this new initiative, we can offer it to those who are in the worst trouble and who may need it the most. Here are some recruitment suggestions:

- Recruit from agencies that have a long-term relationship with clients, agencies that can provide sustained support as the investigators work through their plans. Housing programs, for example, often are engaged with people for as long as two years.

- Work with agencies with positive mental models of people in poverty, agencies that are most likely to share our philosophy.

- Work with organizations that are healthy and rich in resources. The healthier the organization and the more resources it has, the easier it will be for it to change its policies and procedures.

- If possible, recruit people who aren't experiencing a current mental health and/or substance abuse episode.

- Recruit people who want to participate. Using this workbook with coerced people is not recommended. If that becomes necessary, however, it would help if the facilitator were independent of the referring agency.

Whom *not* to work with or recruit from

- Do not recruit from agencies or communities that simply want people in poverty to "behave."

- Do not work with businesses, employers, and corporations that take advantage of employees by paying low wages, use temporary employees almost exclusively, and otherwise exploit people in poverty.

Action phase

When the investigators complete the workbook, the action phase of this process will begin. Putting the plan into action occurs when they leave the class. The transition from your group to the community is crucial to their success, and it's the facilitator's responsibility to prepare the way for the investigators with community agencies and organizations.

Whom to contact

- Agencies that recruited investigators for your group.

- Agencies where investigators are most likely to go for help.

How to contact: Personal contacts are the best. People tend to pay attention to the things they give time to; ask for time to explain the project. Follow-up letters and phone calls will be necessary as the workgroup nears the end of the workbook.

What to cover

- The process and goals for the workbook.

- The possibility that investigators may come to the agencies motivated to change according to their own plans.

- The possibility that investigators may be willing to "partner" with middle-class agencies and middle-class staff members.

- The possibility that investigators may use the hidden rules of class to resolve conflicts with middle-class organizations.

- The possibility that investigators may be able to build enough resources to end their reliance on the agencies.

- The possibility that investigators may be able to join the agency is solving community problems.

What agencies can do to assist *Getting Ahead* investigators?

- Ask about the plans made by the investigators.

- Accept their plans, i.e., work with whatever the investigators bring with them.

- Provide typical resources and services.

- Assign staff who can build relationships of mutual respect.

- Provide connections to new people who can support the investigators. Make room for investigators at the planning tables in the community. People who are typically at the table will need to "move over"—both physically and figuratively. The idea that people from poverty have something of value to share with the group is foreign to some people. It seems that we encounter our "isms" (classism, racism, sexism, and so on) when we're asked to listen to, learn from, and take direction from someone not of our "status." This "giving up of status" can be uncomfortable for people in the dominant culture. If it rankles, check it out. It could be a hidden "ism." As *Getting Ahead* facilitators, we can help facilitate understanding and transformation when we bring people from different classes together.

- Provide long-term persistence in support of the investigators' goals.

WORKBOOK LAYOUT

Fifteen Sessions!

Getting the workbook completed in 15 sessions will be a challenge. The content, duration, and intensity of the workbook should result in it making a lasting impression. Here are some suggestions for getting through the material:

- Meet with each potential investigator individually prior to the first session. Use that time to build a relationship, cover most of the content in Module 1, answer questions, and collect data and signatures.

- Schedule at least 2½ hours for the class so you can work for a full two hours. Take a short break during the session.

- As soon as the investigators grasp the material, move ahead—but encourage them to finish reading the text or do an exercise on their own.

- Assume people won't read much of the text; most of the learning will take place in the group sessions. Use the text as a guide.

- The first time you use the workbook you may need to schedule make-up sessions for people who miss a session to ensure you begin each session with everyone at the same place in the content. In later classes, you will be able to assign the catch-up session to your co-facilitators.

Suggested Schedule of Modules

Some modules will take longer to present than others. Here is a suggested schedule:

SESSION	MODULE
Signing Up/Orientation	Module 1 (portions of)
Session 1	Module 2
	Module 1 (portions of)
Session 2	Module 2, continued
	Module 3
Session 3	Module 4
Session 4	Module 4, continued
Session 5	Module 5
Session 6	Module 5, continued
Session 7	Module 5, continued
	Module 6
Session 8	Module 6, continued
Session 9	Module 7
Session 10	Module 8
Session 11	Module 8, continued
	Module 9
Session 12	Module 9, continued
Session 13	Module 10
	Module 11
Session 14	Module 11, continued
Session 15	Module 11, continued
	Module 12
Celebration	This can be part of the 15th session—or it can be a special gathering

Patterns in the Workbook

Recognizing the patterns in the *Getting Ahead* workbook will help you and the investigators move through it more easily.

A few words about the title *Getting Ahead in a Just-Gettin'-By World: Building Your Resources for a Better Life* ... The idea of "getting ahead" means action and movement—getting ahead of where you once were, not getting ahead of someone else. Survival living is when we are "just gettin' by" every day, which makes it the *world* of someone in poverty. It is also a *political/economic* world, which creates poverty and the just-gettin'-by conditions. The title hints at the discrepancy between what is and what could be. Moving from poverty to economic stability or prosperity doesn't require one to embrace "mad consumerism" or become middle class. It can be done by understanding the rules of money, living simply, and building the resources that Ruby Payne describes.

- Language: The workbook was written in the formal register, with the expectation that the facilitator would translate the information into the casual register as needed. In other words, an investigator does not need to be literate in order to participate. Most of the learning will be done through the development of mental models that the investigators will help create. Investigators will learn the vocabulary and terms needed to be effective in community settings.

- The triangle: Module 1 introduces the triangle that represents all the elements of the workbook. The triangle appears at the beginning of every module thereafter, except for modules 13–15, which are the closing, resources, and reading list. The triangle is to remind the reader which element we're working on: understanding poverty, understanding "where I am," critical thinking and power, responsibility, and planning.

- Learning objectives: A "mediation" table appears at the beginning of each module. It follows the pattern of mediation that we have learned from Dr. Payne: the identification of the stimulus (the what), assigning meaning (the why), and providing a strategy (the how). In *Getting Ahead,* it takes the form of "what's covered" (a mini table of contents for the module), "why it's important" (the why), and "how it's connected to you" (how it can be used). Doing this mediation with the investigators will help organize the information and open a gateway in the brain for learning—the "why-I-should-learn-this" gate.

- The content: The pattern for investigating information has the following elements and headings—information, discussion, activities, and reflections. The order of these is not absolutely consistent. For example, the information and discussion cycles may be repeated before conducting an activity.

  o *Information:* This may take several forms such as filling in the blanks, making lists, drawing mental models, or presentations by the facilitator.

  o *Discussion:* The questions are designed to help people process the information. They are usually worded in such a way as to separate the problem from the person. It isn't necessary to ask and answer every question in the set.

  o *Activities:* The most important activities are the mental models that investigators are asked to create. When the workbook is complete, each person should have a series of mental models that depict his/her life and plans. Some activities take the form of worksheets such as the worksheet on calculating the debt-to-income ratio.

  o *Reflections:* At the end of each module, investigators are asked to think about how this information impacts them personally. It's OK to ask if anyone wants to share his/her insights with the group.

NOTE: Occasionally appearing in a box are quotes or ideas of things to investigate.

FACILITATOR SUPPORT

Tips for Running the Group

- Establish rules that set boundaries and promote respect and safety.

- Establish patterns, rituals, and celebrations.

- Start each session with questions or activities that get everyone to speak so that everyone is established "from the gitgo" as a member of the group that day.

- Be tuned into the mood or underlying feeling in the room. Check with the group if the feeling is not "right."

- Start each session by getting agreement as to the agenda for the day and by discussing time frames.

- From time to time remind the group how many sessions are left. Start working on closure at the sixth or seventh session.

Troubleshooting

One of the best ways we can grow in our work is to share ideas and solve problems together. The aha! Process organization has established a forum for *Getting Ahead* facilitators at www.ahaprocess.com. The password for the forum will be made available at the facilitator training.

Questions and ideas also may be sent directly to Phil DeVol at devol@bright.net.

Evaluation and Research

aha! Process, Inc. also will be gathering data from facilitators for evaluation and research purposes. Facilitators will need to have all investigators complete the forms found in Appendix A, B, and C toward the end of this booklet.

MODULES

Module 1: Getting Started (page 1 in *Getting Ahead*)

Key points

- Module 1 is orientation information that is to be covered in the individual meeting with each member prior to the first group session. The group sessions actually begin with Module 2.

- Use the individual session to begin building your relationship with each investigator and to introduce the unique features of the *Getting Ahead* process. Some of those are:

  o The group is run "kitchen table" style.
  o It's about helping people develop and maintain a stable life.
  o It's an investigation of our own experiences and the community we live in.
  o Everyone in the group is an investigator.
  o People are paid because they are expected to share and produce information that helps them and others.
  o No one tells you what to do.
  o You do a self-assessment so you can develop a plan for yourself.

- Quickly explain how the mediation table at the beginning of each chapter works to show us what is covered in the each module.

- Explain how the triangle works to show the process.

- Work out details on payments.

- Introduce the idea of group rules to establish a sense of safety, but wait to actually create the list of rules until the first *group* session.

- Remember, you can always come back to Module 1 to reinforce patterns.

Supplies and materials
- Forms for collecting basic information
- *Getting Ahead* workbook (you may decide to pass this out in the first session)

Module 2: What It's Like Now (page 7 in *Getting Ahead*)

Key points

- Set up materials, food, room, and table ahead of time, then greet each person before the session begins.

- The sooner you get to listening to the investigators the better. Develop a plan for the first session that includes:

  o Introducing yourself and group members
  o Clarifying expectations
  o Reviewing materials quickly
  o Coming up with group rules

- Go over Learning Objectives (page 7).

- Mental models (page 8): Briefly explain what mental models are and why we use them.

- Background (fill in the blanks): Mental models are **stories, analogies, cartoons, charts, diagrams,** and **drawings.** Mental models are helpful because they help us remember, learn faster, see the whole picture and all its parts, understand complex issues, and not rely on language (written or spoken).

- Use television weather reports to illustrate how mental models help us learn quickly. It would take a long time to talk about everything that we can see in seconds. Big corporations, educators, and social workers use mental models for planning and for dealing with complex concepts.

- On chart paper have the investigators create a mental model of poverty. This is their first experience as investigators. They are the experts on their communities. This is your first opportunity to learn from them. *In Learning to Listen, Learning to Teach* Jane Vella says, "The initial meeting between teacher and learner has to demonstrate the sense of inquiry and curiosity felt by the teacher." This is concrete knowledge. It is valuable because it's how people really experience life. The information the group generates can eventually be used to inform people in positions of power.

- This is the first mental model and a very important one because it's the baseline for all future work. It's also important because you will have to look at it for 15 sessions. It and all following mental models the group develops should be available at every session. Naming and labeling mental models is important because they contain the knowledge of the group; they're the product of the investigation.

- Investigate the parts of the pie—housing, wages, etc.—using the exercises. This is bringing abstract information to the table for the group to analyze in an investigation will reveal key features of the poverty experience. You don't want to draw conclusions for the group, i.e., "give them the answers," but you want to encourage them to think about the meaning of their investigation. Some of the key features of poverty that previous groups have mentioned are:

  o The arithmetic of life doesn't work.
  o Relationships are needed to survive.

- Once you get into the circle it's hard to get out.
- You get stuck living in the moment.
- You don't have much power or influence.
- Many things in the circle are shaky.
- Things in the circle are interconnected.
- You have to go to several agencies in order to survive.
- You have to hustle to make it.

- Investigators will create their own mental model of "What It's Like Now." The title of this mental model is important. Note that it doesn't use the word "poverty"; investigators might not identify with that label. This is a mental model of how things are now in the individual's life. It's important because it's a personal baseline. As you work through the sessions, encourage the investigators to update this mental model. For example, investigators may not put predators in the mental model at first, but when they learn about them they might add them to the model. This is the mental model people will use to examine their own lives. Some investigators will be content with this mental model, while others will look at it and decide they want a different future story. It can be used by the investigators to see the difference between what is and what could be.

- Make sure everyone has drawn a "What It's Like Now" mental model.

- Investigators will need to keep the model because they'll be adding to it and referring to it frequently.

- You want to be neutral and non-judgmental. You don't want to defend or attack individuals *or* the system.

NOTE: This is usually the first place in the sequence of the *Getting Ahead* workbook that people might express a motivation for change. The "aha" moment often comes after the investigators figure out the percentage of their income that goes for housing. When they see that the arithmetic of life isn't working, some people take action immediately.

Supplies and materials
- Chart paper
- Lots of markers
- Inexpensive calculators
- Refreshments
- *Getting Ahead* workbooks
- Paper
- Pens or pencils

Additional reading

Glasmeier, Amy K. (2006). *An Atlas of Poverty in America: One Nation, Pulling Apart, 1960–2003*. New York, NY: Routledge Taylor & Francis Group.

Leondar-Wright, Betsy. (2005). *Class Matters: Cross-Class Alliance Building for Middle-Class Activists*. Gabriola Island, BC: New Society Publishers.

Module 3: Theory of Change (page 19 in *Getting Ahead*)

Key points

The exercises and discussions in this module are designed to make change relevant, to make it something worth thinking about, and to open the topic of change, which is a theme throughout this workbook.

The exercises invite the investigators to examine how agencies address change. This shifts the conversation from the concrete (how are we treated?) to the abstract (what are the theories of the agency?).

This is followed by new information about how people like or don't like to change—the personal side of the topic.

Use the Triangle in Module 1 to explain the *Getting Ahead* theory of change.

A Tool for Facilitators

The following mental model will help you in two ways. First, it will help you see what happens in this workbook; people move from the concrete (the tyranny of the moment) to the abstract and a new future story. Second, it will help you manage the group discussions which can very easily get stuck in story telling.

It's important that you draw the mental models that you see below as you describe the theory of change. It would not be effective to make copies of these models; they must be drawn as you go. You will also want to have them in the group's collection of mental models so you can refer to them as needed.

Here is a step-by-step procedure for developing this mental model.

1. Draw the inner circle and label it "What Life Is Like Now." This represents the mental model that each person drew of their own situation. Have the investigators describe the key features about this life. You want to label this as "Concrete" meaning that it requires people to solve immediate problems all day long and doesn't give them much opportunity to take on abstract issues. This is where we get stuck. Alcoholics, for example, repeat their experiences over and over, finding a way to get high, getting high, getting in trouble, getting over getting in trouble and starting over again. (This discussion reinforces the learning from Module 2 that you just completed.)

2. Draw the outer circle and label it "Abstract." This is new information (what we're looking to discover in this workgroup), education (new ideas), and detachment (when we can see our problems from "outside"). It's easier to go to this space when our lives are stable and we don't have many daily problems. We have time and energy for new things. To get out of the tyranny of the moment and to change our lives we have to be able to get to the abstract.

3. Draw the set of rectangles (representing plans) and the three lines (representing procedural steps) making the point that people in poverty need concrete solutions. Label this "Concrete." When the electricity has been cut off we aren't interested in budgeting information as much as we're interested in getting the heat and lights back on. The discussion here should be about how the immediate concrete solutions are not often effective long-range solutions. We have to get into the abstract to really solve our problems.

4. Now add what goes into the abstract in *Getting Ahead*: Economic Realities (the mental model of poverty and the research on the causes of poverty), the Stages of Change so we can track our own success, and Ruby Payne's information (hidden rules of class, and resources). This is the same information that is in the Triangle, just presented as the *abstract*.

5. Write in the word "PLANS" into set of rectangles and "Procedural Steps" for the three lines below. This is where we begin to emphasize the value of planning and lists.

6. Now talk about how people move from the inner circle to the outer circle, how they cross that thin line. In other words, how do we, when we are stuck in crisis, find a way to get to the abstract? This workbook identified three ways that can be done. One is to use mental models. As we learned in Module 2, mental models can help us see the big picture, connections, relationships, and options—all without a lot of words. The second way is to have someone (a facilitator like you and investigators like them) who can make the information relevant because you know what poverty is like and the hidden rules of class. The third way (the way of this workbook) is to develop a process where people get to explore their lives while learning new information— where they get to see the difference between what is and what can be and develop their own future stories.

This mental model will help you and the group *think* about the progress that is being made. Are we getting to the new information? Are we able to let go of the problems of today enough that we can work on the content of today's investigation?

At the beginning I said this would help you manage the group discussions. You will find that people have a lot to talk about because so many things can go wrong in the course of a week. This mental model can be used to show how, if we keep focused on the problems of today, we will never get to the new information. It is a way the investigators can monitor themselves and keep moving through the material. The level of crisis in the group is something you as the facilitator will want to monitor. There may be times where the demands of the moment simply will not allow for abstract work at all. Should that happen I suggest you visit for a while, eat the donuts, and go home.

Finally, be alert to how people shift from the concrete to the abstract and comment on it. People will be learning metacognition—how to *think about thinking.* The first time this might have happened is when the group investigated the percent of income that went for housing and began to summarize their findings about the mental model of poverty. That is working in the abstract, and it's a joy to see.

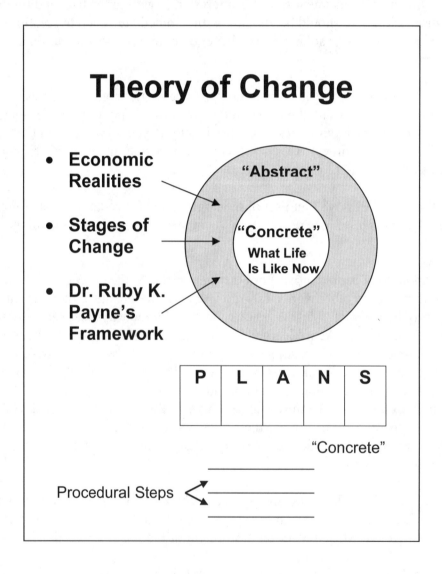

Supplies and materials
- Workbooks
- Chart paper
- Markers
- Pencils, pens

Module 4: The Rich/Poor Gap and How It Works (page 25 in *Getting Ahead*)

Key points

- Our main purpose in exploring the causes of poverty is to illustrate that poverty is about more than the choices of the poor. There are many things that contribute to poverty over which individuals in poverty have no control whatsoever. Of course, it would be better if people came to this conclusion themselves, rather than have the facilitators "teach" it. Another important reason to investigate this information is to give people a way to analyze policies and programs put forward by legislators and social service organizations. Investigators will be able to tell if the policies and programs are comprehensive or if they are focused on one particular cause of poverty.

- Module 4 also can give investigators insight into the mindset of people they encounter at community planning meetings. They will be able to tell who believes that poverty is the result of the choices of the individuals, who believes that it's the result of political/economic structures, who thinks it's a combination of the two, as well as who's aware of predators in the community and who isn't.

- Encourage investigators to think of the strategies that arise out of the research topics. An obvious example would be the research on single parenthood and the strategy of marriage promotion that is offered as a solution.

- Please carefully review the Poverty Research Continuum (Appendix D). It will give you an overview of poverty knowledge supporting this work. To become even more comfortable investigating this information, you will want to read at least one suggested source for each category of research. You'll find it easier to talk about the causes of poverty if you have one solid example for each area of research. See the reading list below for suggestions regarding each area of research.

Additional reading

- Behaviors of the individual

Hart, Betty, & Risley, Todd R. (1995). *Meaningful Differences in the Everyday Experience of Young American Children*. Baltimore, MD: Paul H. Brookes Publishing Co.

Lareau, Annette. (2003). *Unequal Childhoods: Class, Race, and Family Life.* Berkley, CA: University of California Press.

- <u>Human and social capital</u>

Putnam, Robert D. (2000). *Bowling Alone: The Collapse and Revival of American Community.* New York, NY: Simon & Schuster.

Sered, Susan Starr, & Fernandopulle, Rushika. (2005). *Uninsured in America: Life and Death in the Land of Opportunity.* Berkeley, CA: University of California Press.

- <u>Exploitation</u>

Center for Responsible Lending: www.responsiblelending.org.

Lui, Meizhu, Robles, Barbara, Leondar-Wright, Betsy, Brewer, Rose, & Adamson, Rebecca. (2006). *The Color of Wealth: The Story Behind the U.S. Racial Wealth Divide.* New York, NY: The New Press.

- <u>Political/economic structures</u>

Brouwer, Steve. (1998). *Sharing the Pie: A Citizen's Guide to Wealth and Power in America.* New York, NY: Henry Holt & Company.

Kelly, Marjorie. (2001). *The Divine Right of Capital: Dethroning the Corporate Aristocracy.* San Francisco, CA: Berrett-Koehler Publishers.

Following is a short list for each of the four areas of research. These entries can be used to help fill in the tables on page 27 of the *Getting Ahead* workbook.

- <u>Behaviors of individuals in poverty</u>

  - An obvious example would be the research on single parenthood and the strategy of marriage promotion that is offered as a solution.
  - Encourage investigators to think of the strategies that arise out of the research topics. An obvious example would be the research on single parenthood and the strategy of marriage promotion that is offered as a solution.
  - Poor choices made by the individual
  - Single parenthood
  - Addiction and/or mental illness
  - Literacy or lack thereof

- <u>Human skills and social systems</u>

  - Lack of good-paying jobs
  - Lack of high-quality educational opportunities

- o Decline of neighborhoods
- o Suburbanization of manufacturing
- o Failure of social services
- o Lack of career ladder between service and knowledge sector

- Exploitation

  - o Coal mining in Appalachia
  - o Poor-paying jobs
  - o Companies that (1) don't give employees enough hours to have benefits and (2) expect the government to subsidize their business
  - o Communities that engage in the "race to the bottom"
  - o Payday lenders, cash-advance outlets
  - o Lease/purchase operations

- Political/economic structures

  - o Corporate influence over legislators
  - o Tax structures that favor the corporations and the wealthy
  - o Declining wages
  - o De-industrialization
  - o Broken management/labor "bargain"

Other observations about Module 4:

- The Predator worksheet on page 29 is important because it forms a concrete list that can add accurate information to each individual's "What It's Like Now" mental model. Encourage the investigators to not only identify predators but to identify exactly how the predators work.

- The information on economic disparity is very abstract information. Using mental models and activities from United for a Fair Economy will help make it meaningful (Appendix F). Groups usually enjoy these exercises. It isn't necessary to do every exercise in Appendix F. Make the points and move on.

- Who pays the most tax? This section should be addressed only after reading Ruby Payne's article, "Where Do We Go from Here? How Do Communities Develop Intellectual Capital and Sustainability?" (Appendix G). Her approach brings the discussion of economic issues to a community level that is non-ideological and safe. The point here is to help the investigators see how all three classes are impacted by the current economic situation.

- Investigators will be making mental models of what life is like for the middle class and for those from wealth. The activity calls for the investigators to read the stories and draw the mental models. You might consider reading the stories before the session and paraphrasing the stories for the group. These mental models are very important because you will be using them to illustrate where the hidden rules of middle class and wealth come from. These will become part of the group's collection of mental model. This is also an opportunity to build a future story that includes all three classes (poverty, middle class, and wealth) working together to create a sustainable community.

- The "Community Sustainability Grid" in Appendix H is being used in several cities to guide planning. You may choose to introduce this to the group, particularly if you are working with people of color or the investigators express an interest in broad community issues. Here are some key points about the grid:

  o The grid is a mental model that presents two themes: (1) We must develop strategies that cover all four areas of research on the causes of poverty. These are listed across the top of the grid as column headings. (2) Creating a sustainable community will require the engagement of individuals, organizations (agencies, schools, health care providers, courts, etc.), the community (elected leaders, business sector, faith-based entities, and cultural groups), and changes in policies. These are labeled in the left-hand column.

  o The grid works best as a planning tool. It doesn't work as a way to list current activities. Putting words in the squares gives the *appearance* of coverage that may be misleading. For example, to say Early Head Start is available in the community might give the impression that early-childhood needs are being addressed, but the fact is that Head Start serves less than 3% of eligible children.

  o As a planning tool it can be used to talk about what an individual might do in each area. For example, **Individual Action** (first row) might be filled in this way across the continuum: An individual might volunteer to teach budgeting to people in poverty. That would be addressing "individual behavior." If a person volunteered with Habitat for Humanity to build houses, he/she would be addressing "human and social capital." If someone volunteered to do tax returns for people in poverty so they could utilize the Earned Income Tax Credit, he/she would be addressing "exploitation" because the individual in poverty could avoid the predatory lending that accompanies the so-called instant returns. And if an individual writes letters to the editor or legislators about poverty/prosperity issues, he/she would be addressing "political/economic structures."

  o **Organizational Action** (second row) can be used to identify the focus of a particular organization or agency in terms of the causes of poverty. Does the agency focus on:

    - Changing the behavior of the individual?
    - Improving financial, human, and social capital in the community?

- Addressing predators?
- Policy, programming, and systemic issues?

One of the important lessons to be learned from using this grid is that most social services, healthcare, workforce development, or court programs are focused on changing the thinking and behaviors of the individual. That in itself is worthy work. Indeed, it's important for individuals to be given the help they need to work on their future stories, to practice choice making, to become accountable to themselves and others, to get healthier, and to become self-directed learners.

o Organizational Action also can include work in the second column, "human and social capital," if it works at changing policies and practices to improve services and outcomes in cooperation with other community organizations. Individuals in poverty use the services and programs of many community organizations in order to survive their unstable environment. Organizations might plan and develop a sophisticated service-delivery model by building partnerships or collaboratives that can improve outcomes for people in poverty.

o Most organizations do not address exploitation that their clients face, and very few address political/economic structures. In other words, the focus of most entities working on poverty/prosperity issues is narrow. Which brings us to another point about the organizational action row …

o Society has given the work of ending poverty to community organizations to solve. Schools are meant to produce children with the skill sets necessary to compete in a knowledge-sector environment. Workforce-development agencies are to make people ready for the workplace. Healthcare organizations are to keep the population healthy. The criminal-justice system is to reduce recidivism. The work of ending poverty cannot be separated from the work of building prosperity—and that cannot be done by the social-service sector. The research on the causes of poverty makes it quite plain that poverty is caused by a wide array of factors that are far beyond the relatively narrow scope of Organizational Action. No amount of federal or state money, no innovation or management technique applied to or by the social sector will build sustainable communities. To continue to insist on that as a solution will produce nothing but the results we're getting now. This brings us to the third row, **Community Action.**

o Building prosperity and sustainability will require action at the community level. Businesses, elected officials, faith-based entities, and all cultural groups must be brought into the planning and the action. On the grid, Community Action can address the causes of poverty that fall under the headings of human and social capital, exploitation, and political/economic structures. According to the *World Development Report 2006: Equity and Development* put out by the World Bank, the best economic growth does not come from focusing on growth alone and trusting that most people attain a high quality of life. It comes from both growth *and* equity. Communities must, at the very least, provide four forms of equity in order for communities to experience prosperity. These are a fair shot (equity) at:

- A well-paying job
- Good healthcare
- Good education
- Fair credit

Communities that use the grid will involve all sectors of the community (and all three classes) to create the political and economic will to foster the necessary infrastructure, incentives, and opportunities. As noted above, the business community must be involved in this effort. One community has a steering committee that intentionally addresses the Community Action row. It has confronted predatory lending practices in the community and offered typical banking services to people in poverty by working with local banks and credits unions. Other communities are engaging business leaders, who already have a commitment to the community, in this work. It should be remembered that there have always been business leaders who embrace a larger sense of community well-being as part of their mission. The annual November issue of *Fortune* magazine lists the 100 best companies to work for. Those companies don't focus entirely on the bottom line; they also treat their employees well and contribute to their communities. In other words, there are in fact many business leaders who already share the value of strong, prosperous communities and understand the important role of business in their creation.

o Some investigators will want to participate at the community level, have their voices heard, or be at the planning table. This grid can be a great help to them because it frames the work of community sustainability, poverty, and prosperity in a broad way. It gives them the ability to analyze the proposals brought to the table, and it can give them insight into the mindsets of the other people at the table. For example:

- "That man is coming from the point of view that poverty is about the choices of the poor."
- "That woman thinks that poverty is a systemic issue."

o The fourth row, **Policy Change,** is the most abstract and therefore the most difficult to develop plans for. Not only are policies beyond the immediate influence of most people in middle class and poverty, the time horizon for working on them is likely to be one or two decades. And yet, it's vital that we address policy issues.

o   First, it needs to be understood that we're already being driven by policy—in very concrete terms. For example, the Welfare Reform Act of 1996 is the driving force that determines the policies, programs, and procedures of many governmental and non-governmental organizations that work with people in poverty. That legislation is focused almost entirely on the first area of research, the behaviors of the individual. For example, the introductory language of that act refers to research on the correlation between single parenthood and the break up of families and poverty. That driving force created the policy of "work first," with less emphasis on education. It created time limits that remove people from the welfare rolls but not from poverty. On the other hand, President Lyndon Johnson's War on Poverty in the 1960s was focused more on community factors and political/economic causes of poverty. The ongoing discourse on poverty swings with the political winds and is often presented in either/or terms. One side says poverty is caused by the choices of the poor and virtually nothing else. It's "this" and not "that." The other side says it's caused by political/economic structures that result in downward pressure on wages and economic disparity and virtually nothing else. The fact is that poverty is caused *both* by the choices of the poor and political/economic structures *and* everything in between (including exploitation and human and social capital). What our communities need is not the shallow *either/or* thinking debates, but *both/and* thinking that brings everyone to the table for a true dialogue.

o   We are now in a period of extreme distrust of government. People in government itself and in the private sector don't value the role of social/economic policies. The best way to understand the value of policy as it applies to the construction of prosperity and a high quality of life is to examine how the middle class was created in the United States. Consider the following seven points:

1.   The U.S. was able to create the middle-class farmer. The economic stability farmers enjoyed, the wealth they created and passed on to their children, and their prosperity did not come from their labor alone. It came largely from government policies and sponsorship, such as the Homestead Act of 1862, which gave farmers 60 acres from which to make a start. Slave labor created wealth for the owners; in 1850 the income of the average slave owner in South Carolina was 10 times that of the average income of other whites in the state. In 1848 Mexico lost half its territory to the United States, and in 1851 the Sioux tribe gave up the entire state of Iowa to the U.S. All these policies and governmental actions created wealth for the agricultural middle class.

2.   The industrial middle class did not earn its stability, prosperity, and wealth through its paycheck alone. Government policies protected workers by cutting off "Oriental" immigration and, after World War I, immigration from Europe. Additionally, children were removed from the workplace by

child-labor laws, and the "family wage" increased income for married men. Henry Ford improved wages because he wanted employees to be able to own the cars they made. Later, unionization introduced the 40-hour work week, higher wages, and job security. With government support, employers provided employer-based health insurance.

3. The white-collar "Leave It to Beaver" middle class was created by tax codes that encouraged employers to provide employer-based health insurance and employer-based pensions. After World War II, the GI Bill provided education, student loans, and home mortgages. Government policies also created Social Security and Medicare—and paid for the roads, highways, and infrastructure that supported home ownership and the growth of the suburbs.

4. The wealth that was created by these policies and that was passed down to subsequent generations did not extend to all. In *The Color of Wealth*, published by United for a Fair Economy in 2006, the authors explain the wealth divide in the United States. Agrarian middle-class opportunities were reserved almost exclusively for whites—and often at the direct expense of people of color. During the 1850s the land made available to whites was taken from Native Americans in a series of battles, appropriations, and treaties. And while whites accumulated wealth from slave labor, Mexicans lost their land to the U.S. Only whites were eligible for California land claims during the Gold Rush; the "Foreign Miner's Tax" of 1850 stopped Mexicans from participating in the Gold Rush. This policy was extended to the Chinese in 1852.

5. Industrial and white-collar middle-class opportunities also were largely limited to whites. Black colleges couldn't accommodate all the returning black veterans wanting to use the GI Bill, which left the black veterans with no place to go for higher education, as most colleges were still segregated. From 1930 to 1960 only 1% of all mortgages were issued to African Americans. Japanese Americans who lost property while interned received just 10 cents on the reparation dollar. In Puerto Rico (a territory of the U.S.), most locally owned businesses were crowded out by U.S. companies when Operation Bootstrap gave them tax incentives in 1947. During World War II, Mexicans were brought to the U.S. to fill labor shortages and then deported in Operation Wetback. In the 1950s Congress "terminated" recognition of certain Native American tribes, thus throwing the prosperous Menominee and Klamath tribes into poverty.

6. The legacies of wealth and poverty still persist—and despite the civil-rights laws of the 1960s, discrimination still exists in the United States. Racism may not seem overt, and institutional racism has abated somewhat, but there is still a huge benefit to being white and a cost to being of color. Those who think we need not talk about color, race, and diversity are

expressing a color-blindness not supported by the facts. For example, the *racial wealth gap* continues to grow. According to the U.S. Federal Reserve Bank, the median net worth (assets minus debts) of families of color dropped 7% from 1995 to 2001, from $17,900 to $17,100. During the same period the net worth of white families grew 37%, from $103,400 to $120,900.

7. Finally, it should be noted that the middle class is shrinking for the first time in U.S. history. The very policies and structures that made the middle class are disappearing, including employer-based healthcare, employer-based pensions, the 40-hour work week, wages, student loans, mortgage assistance, and Social Security.

We undertook this discussion about the middle class to emphasize the importance that policy has on our direct experience of life. Laws passed by Congress and decisions made by the Judiciary have an impact on the economy. Policies work for people at the bottom of the ladder, low-wage workers, and the middle class or they work against them. The free market and the economy do not operate in a vacuum, but are molded by policy. Policy is important to the creation of sustainable communities.

So, it is indeed, that poverty is caused by the choices of the poor, and political economic structures and everything in between—community resources and exploitation.

The key point about the Community Sustainability Grid: The wider and the deeper we go in the grid the better our plans will be.

This module is another point in the sequence of *Getting Ahead* at which people have begun making their own arguments for change. They are beginning to shape a future story for themselves in which they play a role in community discussion.

Supplies and materials
- Workbooks
- Chart paper
- Markers
- Pencils, pens
- Lots of space to move about: park, gym, parking lot

See Appendix F regarding specific supplies for the exercises you choose to use.

Additional reading

Lind, Michael. (2004) Are We Still a Middle-Class Nation? *The Atlantic*. Volume 293, No. 1, January-February; pages 120–128.

Lui, Meizhu, Robles, Barbara, Leondar-Wright, Betsy, Brewer, Rose, & Adamson, Rebecca. (2006) *The Color of Wealth: The Story Behind the U.S. Racial Wealth Divide*. New York, NY: The New Press.

World Bank. (2005). *World Development Report 2006: Equity and Development*. New York, NY: Oxford University Press.

Module 5: Hidden Rules of Economic Class (page 43 in *Getting Ahead*)

Key points

- Define hidden rules as the unwritten cues and habits of groups. These rules come from the environment in which a child is raised. For example, survival living, as described by the "What It's Like Now" mental model, generates the hidden rules of poverty.

- If investigators see the hidden rules of poverty as a description of their status *only*, we will have failed. Our job is to present the hidden rules as the understandable rules of class—poverty, middle class, and wealth—in a neutral, non-judgmental way and allow the process of this workbook to unfold.

- Investigators may think that they are being labeled when they first learn about the hidden rules. It isn't your job to defend the material in the workbook or to persuade the investigators to accept the hidden rules. However, it is your job to help the investigators to *investigate* the information. If you encounter resistance to the ideas, cover them generally and give people a few days to see if hidden rules don't actually play out around them.

- In this workbook it's important to reinforce information again and again throughout the 15 sessions, and "hidden rules" is one topic that needs to be revisited often. When the investigators gather for each session, as well as before the sessions begin, listen for stories the participants tell. Some of the stories, particularly those about their experiences with agencies and the workplace, will be about hidden rules. Actually, many of the stories will be about how rules were broken. Using their own examples to teach the rules and analyze the situations they find themselves in will help the learning process.

- Our goal is to help the investigators be able to choose which hidden rules to use while building resources. The investigators have not yet been introduced to resources (that comes in the next module), but it isn't too early for you to be listening for the connections in their lives between hidden rules and resources. For example, when parents have run-ins with schools they often defend their children by attacking the teachers or principal and using the casual register. The hidden rules being used (protecting children and the casual register) actually work against building mental (educational) resources for children. Investigators can discuss the value of using formal-register language to negotiate to get support for children from the school system.

- Be sure to cover the KEY POINTS TO REMEMBER on page 44 (not to be confused with *these* key points). It's easy to insult people with the information on hidden rules. Emphasize that this work is based on patterns—and there are many exceptions to these patterns. Stay focused on economic realities and how these patterns arise out of poverty and not the other way around.

- Explore how conflict arises as a result of some rules. We want to use our knowledge of the hidden rules to resolve conflicts. Ask group members to list ways they can use the information right away.

- While investigating the hidden rules, slip in concrete applications to whet the appetite for more information. For example, Robert Kiyosaki's book *Rich Dad, Poor Dad* has mental models of how people in poverty, middle class, and wealth think of money. These can be taught in just a few minutes. (You don't want this to turn into a long session on money management.) For copyright reasons, we can't provide those mental models here, so interested facilitators will want to buy Kiyosaki's book. The mental models can be found in Chapter 3, Lesson 2.

- When looking into the hidden rule for time, have the investigators draw several mental models for time. This reinforces the theme of "time" in this workbook. We introduced the concept of the "tyranny of the moment" when we built the mental model of poverty in Module 2, then talked about getting to the abstract in Module 3. Here you can make the point again that people who are stuck in the tyranny of the moment often think and talk about the present and the past, but spend less time thinking about the future. When you talk about time, it's helpful to draw a time line that shows all three. Let group members come up with models of their own. One group used the "Slinky" as a model for time because of the ups and downs that occur for people in poverty. For example, it often takes a student from a poverty situation four years to get through a two-year degree program because his/her environment tends to be unstable and vulnerable. Students from a stable environment can usually get through a four-year degree program in four years.

- Discuss in detail the hidden rule on power; it will be one of the favorites. Illustrate how people will quit jobs over this rule and tie this rule to the rule on time. People who use reactive strategies to solve problems (the supervisor has insulted you, so to keep your dignity and pride you feel you have to quit)—and who aren't oriented to the future—will often walk off the job.

- The purpose of the exercise on hidden rules and public policy on page 61 is to illustrate concretely that the powerful and wealthy generally set public policy. The first arrow should go from the wealthy to the middle class, the second from the middle class to poverty. This may seem simplistic, but we need to present this in the form of a mental model in order to aid memory. This brief exercise reinforces the concepts on policy introduced with the Community Sustainability Grid introduced in Module 4.

- This is *not* about confronting people over their hidden rules that interfere with change or healthy behavior. Don't criticize the hidden rules of any class; they are used to survive in that environment. We simply offer two other sets of rules, thus providing more options.

- If you find yourself getting defensive, hear yourself "preaching," or sense that you're getting angry, you're allowing your emotions to hijack you, which will be counterproductive for the group as well. Take a break and identify the value that you hold dear that was being challenged, then let go of it. During this process all investigators will make their own assessment of their situation, prioritize what they want to work on, and then make their plans.

Supplies and materials
- Workbooks
- Chart paper
- Markers
- Pencils, pens

Additional reading

Alexie, Sherman. (1993). *The Lone Ranger and Tonto Fistfight in Heaven*. New York, NY: HarperPerennial. [Interesting insights into time can be found on pages 21–22 of this book.]

Fussell, Paul. (1983). *Class: A Guide Through the American Status System*. New York, NY: Touchstone.

Galeano, Eduardo. (1998). *Upside Down: A Primer for the Looking-Glass World*. New York, NY: Metropolitan Books.

Jain, Anjali. (2001.) Why don't low-income mothers worry about their preschoolers being overweight? *Pediatrics*. Volume 107, pages 1138–1145. [Hidden rules on food get as close to identity and belonging as one can get. What and how people eat is very difficult to change, as health professionals have learned when trying to impact obesity, stress-related diseases, and cardiovascular illness. The Jain study found that most low-income mothers didn't accept the medical standards on obesity and defined their children's weight by their own perceptions. Those who did try to change their eating habits were sometimes overridden by other family members or by their own impulse to show love to their children in the ways they fed them.]

Module 6: Eleven Resources (page 63 in *Getting Ahead*)

Key points

- Up until now we have been co-investigating research and hidden rules, which are systemic issues and generalizations. As much as they apply to our sense of identity and belonging, they are generally easier to talk about than what we will be doing next. The test groups found relief in the research because they learned that poverty was *not* just about them, that large systemic issues were at work. The hidden rules also were amusing; it was fun to explore the behaviors of the three economic groups.

- In this module you will be introducing a core concept, a foundational component of this work. This is where we define poverty and prosperity; what is learned now will be used to make plans at the end of the workbook.

- Resources can be defined as quality-of-life indicators. Intuitively, taking the 11 resources as a whole, it's better to have high resources than low resources. It would be fair to say that a high quality of life does not depend on having high financial resources, but it's also fair to say that being financially stable reduces stress and lightens the future.

- People in poverty *tend* to have lower resources than others. In fact, that is one definition of poverty: the extent to which a person does without resources. This is made easier to understand and accept when we remember the mental model of poverty that we created in Module 2. Being poor in the U.S. means that we're vulnerable to daily fears and problems to the extent that we're living in the tyranny of the moment. We don't have enough time to solve daily problems, let alone build financial, emotional, mental, or social resources.

- So assessing the resources of individuals is difficult—even painful—to do. This is about the individual, and every investigator will have a different story, different strengths, and different weaknesses. Working on this is reminiscent of the typical agency assessment experience where people are more likely to be defined as "needy and deficient" and handed a treatment plan. Naturally, we want to avoid that experience altogether.

- In this module the investigators will be scoring (assessing) case studies because we want to practice using the concepts that we'll use later when we do a self-assessment of our own resources.

- The chart titled "Resource Scoring Table," which appears on page 75 of Module 6 of the workbook, introduces five definitions for each resource, ranging from "Urgent/Crisis" to "Thriving/Giving Back." These are numbered 1 to 5 where 1 is low and 5 is high. In Module 8 these definitions and scoring mechanisms will appear in the self-assessment in an expanded format. Take a moment to go to Module 8 to see the expanded version of this table. You'll notice that for each box in this table there's a series of statements. You need not use the detailed scoring statements of Module 8 here in Module 6, but it's important that you know that we're introducing an idea and process here that will be reinforced later.

- Use the case studies from Chapter 1 in *Bridges Out of Poverty* or case studies that you create to practice the scoring of resources. *Always* focus on the strengths a person has within each resource and across all resources. After all, it's upon *strengths* that plans for economic stability are built.

- Most investigators tend to make sweeping (sometimes oversimplified) appraisals of the case studies and their own resources. To confront an investigator's rationale for his/her thinking is too much like school with all of its "right" answers. It would be better to work over the material several times, using more and more precise questions to help people make accurate assessments of their own resources.

- If or when you start to "lose" the group—when they start getting caught up in their feelings, looking down, growing silent, or flat getting defensive—stop and take a break.

- Remind the group of your timeline. You're going to be meeting for 15 sessions. How many sessions remain? This is important because it illustrates how to think of time, and it begins to work toward closure.

Supplies and materials
- Case studies copied from *Bridges Out of Poverty*
- Workbooks
- Chart paper
- Markers
- Pencils, pens

Additional reading

Andreas, Steve, & Faulkner, Charles. (Eds.). (1994). *NLP: The New Technology of Achievement*. New York, NY: Quill. [Note: NLP stands for neurolinguistic programming.]

Covey, Stephen R. (1989). *The Seven Habits of Highly Effective People: Powerful Lessons in Personal Change*. New York, NY: Fireside Book, Simon & Schuster.

Goleman, Daniel. (1995). *Emotional Intelligence*. New York, NY: Bantam Books.

Putnam, Robert D. (2000). *Bowling Alone: The Collapse and Revival of American Community*. New York, NY: Simon & Schuster.

Module 7: Stages of Change (page 79 in *Getting Ahead*)

Key points

- This module adds to the discussion on motivation in the previous chapter.

- Our goal is to help people gain power in their lives by taking charge of and monitoring their own changes.

- It's important for investigators to know that the stages of change almost never occur in a straight line and that relapse is normal. The point is that when there is a relapse we don't have to start all over but can go back the preparation or action stage.

- This module is the only module that can be taught out of sequence. It only takes a short time to cover and can be put into a previous session whenever time permits.

Supplies and materials
- Workbooks
- Chart paper
- Markers
- Pencils, pens

Additional reading

Miller, William R., & Rollnick, Stephen. (2002). *Motivational Interviewing: Preparing People for Change* (Second Edition). New York, NY: Guilford Press.

Module 8: Self-Assessment Regarding Resources (page 83 in *Getting Ahead*)

Key points

- The investigators know the importance of this module. Some people will be apprehensive about doing it, even dreading it. You will be banking on your relationship with each other for support on this day. Remind the investigators that they have been doing solid, analytical thinking—tight thinking—during all their investigations, so they simply need to continue doing what they've been doing.

- The quality of the self-assessments will determine the quality of the plans, so it's important that people come to it prepared.

- People in generational poverty are likely to have low resources. Some individuals in the test groups went through the process, looked at their low scores, and began to revise them upward—thus the eight-point procedural steps preceding the self-assessment. Encourage investigators to resist the urge to "improve" their scores.

- At the end of the Module 8 process the investigators will have a mental model—a bar chart—depicting their resources.

- This is another point in the sequence of the workbook where people might express their motivation for change. It can be very painful. One woman reported that she went to the bathroom and wept for 20 minutes before she returned with a determination to build her own resources and their resources of her children.

Supplies and materials
- Workbooks
- Chart paper
- Markers
- Pencils, pens

Module 9: Building Resources (page 103 in *Getting Ahead*)

Key points

- Remind the group of how many sessions are left and attempt to estimate the amount of work that lies ahead. This also continues the work toward closure.

- Treat this module like any other; it's an investigation. Do **not** have local agencies come in to tell the group about their services and programs, unless the investigators come up with that idea themselves and have general agreement in the group to do so. When investigators dig out where and how to raise resources it will be more powerful than listening to agency "dog and pony shows."

- Resources come from three places: communities, families, and individual action. Strong, healthy communities that can deliver well-paying jobs, good healthcare, good schools, and fair credit (reinforcing what was covered in Module 4) can help families build the resources of their children. Healthy, motivated families can pass on more than financial wealth to their children; they can pass on emotional, spiritual, social, and mental assets too. Individuals can choose to build their own resources and the quality of their lives. Sometimes it's as simple as going to a bookstore and getting into the non-fiction section. There are current books on how to build every one of the 11 resources.

- The building of resources reinforces the information in Module 4 about the causes of poverty. Once again, it takes work on the part of the individual, the agencies, the community, and those developing policy.

- Start with the premise that we will use our higher resources to build up our lower resources.

- Everyone's story and everyone's self-assessment of resources will be different, so we need to help each other think of ways to build all 11 resources.

- The tic-tac-toe method will produce more possible solutions than simple brainstorming, but it takes longer.

- The names of many agencies that appeared earlier when we were talking about the righting reflex and "Whose plan is it?" will appear again. There may be mixed feelings about this because of past experiences with the agencies, but this is the opportunity to reframe the relationship between the participant and the agency. The shift in motivation and power makes all the difference. Imagine a participant going to an agency as a result of his/her own assessment—with the determination and a plan to build a particular resource. The motivation and power would now lie with the participant.

- It's in this exercise that it becomes very apparent that hidden rules can be a choice. Investigators will discuss the relative value of which rules to use. Middle-class rules sometimes will not be the only or best choice.

- This is when a partnership between middle-class agency personnel and the investigators can be fostered.

- This is also when we can introduce the idea of transition. We can either stay where we are, doing what we normally do, or we can begin a transition toward whatever it is we want. With the tools discussed in this module, we can start to define the steps between what we have now and what we see in the future. Whatever our setting, we can help each other make the transition across economic class lines.

- Further, this is when hidden rules can be used to resolve conflicts and improve outcomes. There are four ways in which the hidden rules work:

  1. When neither party (middle class or poverty) is aware of or intentional in the use of the hidden rules. This applies in the vast majority of interactions.

  2. When the middle-class person is aware of and intentional in the use of the rules, and the person in poverty is not. This tends to be limited to those who have attended an aha! Process workshop or read aha! Process books.

  3. When the person in poverty is aware of and intentional in the use of the rules and the person in middle class is not. This also tends to be limited to those who have attended an aha! Process workshop, read aha! Process books, or participated in a *Getting Ahead* group.

  4. When both the middle-class person and the person in poverty are aware of and intentional in the use of the hidden rules. This applies to very few people indeed … so far!

Supplies and materials
- Workbooks
- Chart paper
- Markers
- Pencils, pens

Module 10: Community Assessment (page 109 in *Getting Ahead*)

Key points

- This module turns the investigation back to the community and away from the focus on ourselves. It comes at a good time; the investigators may be tired from the rigorous self-assessment.

- In this module we reinforce the work done in Module 2 (where we examined wages and housing conditions), Module 4 (where we investigated all the causes of poverty), and Module 9 (where we discovered where in our community to go to build resources). We must be consistent about not putting the onus for action on people in poverty alone.

- This also is an opportunity for investigators to become problem solvers in the community. For example, they may choose to advocate for improved housing, better-paying jobs, fair credit opportunities, or to become facilitators for United for a Fair Economy. They may choose to partner with middle-class people on issues like land use and school issues. In addition, one of the investigators may become your co-facilitator for the next *Getting Ahead* workshop.

- If there's enough time, you may want to invite community advocates and leaders to meet with the investigators to help them assess how well the community is dealing with poverty and prosperity issues. It's less important that the co-investigators look for strengths; agency folks will typically frame their information that way. On the other hand, our goal is to build a partnership between people in poverty and the middle class. So it might be wise to create some guidelines for the interviews with group members and to debrief the experience afterward in the context of what they've learned in *Getting Ahead*. In such meeting should be seen as the beginning of the relationship, not just an opportunity for one meeting with community leaders. Our hope is to assist investigators who want to become involved to the decision-making tables in the community.

- As part of their plan, some investigators may want to do more research on community resources.

- The investigators should create a single Community Assessment Mental Model (bar chart) to share with community leaders. In fact, all the information that the investigators create in the workbook is concrete information that needs to be shared.

Additional reading

Miringoff, Marc, & Miringoff, Marque-Luisa. (1999). *The Social Health of the Nation: How America Is Really Doing*. New York, NY: Oxford University Press. [Dr. Marc Miringoff's lecture on the Social Health Index provides an interesting way to measure and monitor a community's health. It can be found at www.jrn.columbia.edu/events/census/presenters/miringoff/index.asp.]

NOTE: The idea of sustainability introduced in Module 4 can be enhanced in the module if there is time. Interesting mental models on the subject can be found at www.sustainablemeasures.com.

Supplies and materials
- Workbooks
- Chart paper
- Markers
- Pencils, pens

Module 11: Your Plan for Getting from Poverty to Prosperity (page 117 in *Getting Ahead*)

Key points

- As we know, living on the bottom rungs of the economic ladder forces people into a reactive way of solving problems, so don't assume that investigators have experience in planning or working through procedural steps. Follow the steps in the workbook all the way through.

- Do *not* present this as homework. If people don't do it, they're less likely to come to the next session.

- Do *not* stress the "individual" nature of the plan. That would be too much like a test. Present it as something the group will do. Allow people to talk and share while working on their plans.

- Investigators may want and need feedback from you. While group members are working on their plans, you may offer to meet with people individually to talk over their plans. This is the only time you will want to play the role of critic and adviser—and only when you've been asked. The questions and issues you raise may spur deeper and tighter thinking.

- These plans are one of the major goals of this effort, but to over-emphasize them may backfire. It's better to treat the plans as part of a low-key celebration, something that people want to join in.

- Investigators will create a support team to help them over the long term. Any assistance the agencies and community can provide should be identified. The more concrete the tie between the individual and the various members of the team and community the better.

- Keep working toward closure, reminding investigators that the group sessions are almost over. Ask if there's anything special they would like to do at the last meeting.

Additional reading

Botelho, Richard J. (2002). Beyond advice: 1. Becoming a motivational practitioner. Available at www.motivationalinterview.org

Botelho, R.J. (2002). Motivate healthy habits: using self-guided change methods. www.MotivateHealthyHabits.com

Miller, William R., & Rollnick, Stephen. (2002). *Motivational Interviewing: Preparing People for Change* (Second Edition). New York, NY: Guilford Press.

Miller, W.R. (2000). Appendix B: Screening and assessment instruments. In: Enhancing motivation for change in substance abuse treatment, SAMHSA Treatment Improvement Protocol (TIP) Series 35, DHHS Publication No. (SMA) 00-3460, pages 220–225. Rockville, MD: Center for Substance Abuse Treatment.

Supplies and materials
- Workbooks
- Chart paper
- Markers
- Pencils, pens

Module 12: Creating Mental Models for Your Personal Path Out of Poverty *and* for Community Prosperity (page 131 in *Getting Ahead*)

Key points

- The plans created in the previous module are in worksheet form. All the details should be there, but as worksheets they will not be easy to remember. The goal of this module is to present those plans in the form of a mental model.

- Allow people to work individually and in groups. Challenge them to build on each others' ideas, to squeeze in more and more meaning, to represent all aspects of their plans.

- Stop the group action from time to time to have people report to spur new thinking.

- Finally, create a mental model for community prosperity. What would it take? Who would have to be involved? How long would it take? In Appendix E you will find an example of a mental model created by a group in Mount Vernon, Ohio (see Acknowledgments in *Getting Ahead* workbook).

This brings together the two themes of *Getting Ahead:* the personal examination of the investigator's life, as well as a personal plan for the community aspect of building resources and prosperity.

The final mental model is another product of the group that can be of value to other community members.

A good mental model will:

- Include all important elements.
- Identify time frames or time lines that show the past, present, and future.
- Show the distinctions between individual and community responsibility.
- Show the relative importance of the different parts.
- Show the relationships between people.
- Identify the key players.
- Show options and possible consequences.

This activity can be fun. Enjoy it!

Supplies and materials
- Workbooks
- Chart paper
- Markers
- Pencils, pens
- Celebration materials

Module 13: Closing and Transition (page 137 in *Getting Ahead*)

Key points

- There needs to be a formal closing for the workshop—something that is fun, allows people to express feelings, shows appreciation, and says goodbye.

- The closing celebration would do well to include the idea that this is really the beginning of something new.

- Briefly discuss everyone's future story. What is the first thing you're going to do? What do you think your life will be like a year from now? Who will you involve in the changes you make?

- Two evaluations must be conducted at the end of the experience: one to measure satisfaction with the workshop itself and another to measure the stage of change for each investigator.

APPENDIX

A. Participant Data Sheet

B. Roster and Attendance

C. Post-Workbook Participant Evaluation and Stages of Change Assessment

D. Poverty Research Continuum

E. Mental Model for Creating Individual and Community Prosperity

F. Material from *The Growing Divide* (United for a Fair Economy)
    Activity 4: Income Quintiles
    Activity 6: The CEO Pay Gap
    Activity 7: The 10 Chairs

G. "Where Do We Go from Here? How Do Communities Develop Intellectual Capital and Sustainability?" by Ruby K. Payne, Ph.D.

H. Community Sustainability Grid

I. Model Fidelity Elements

J. *Getting Ahead* Facilitator Qualities

NAME:	PHONE:	SEX: M F AGE: RACE:
ADDRESS: PARENTS' OR GRANDPARENTS' ADDRESS:		NUMBER IN HOUSEHOLD: NUMBER OF CHILDREN IN HOUSEHOLD:
CURRENT WORK STATUS: (circle one) Unemployed Employed at two or more places Employed part time Employed full time	HOURLY WAGE OF MOST RECENT JOB:	NUMBER OF JOBS HELD IN PAST 12 MONTHS:
EDUCATIONAL LEVEL: (circle highest level completed) Some high school High school diploma or GED Some college courses College degree Some graduate classes Graduate degree	OTHER TRAINING: (circle completed courses) Goal setting Computers Parenting Money management Résumé writing Budgeting Communication Other (explain): _____ _____	
INCOME:	ALCOHOL/DRUG TREATMENT:	MENTAL HEALTH COUNSELING:
STAGE OF CHANGE: ___ Pre-Contemplation ___ Contemplation ___ Preparation ___ Action ___ Maintenance		

Getting Ahead in a Just-Gettin'-By World
Participant Data Sheet

Appendix B

Getting Ahead in a Just-Gettin'-By World
Attendance: left column—date of the session. Initial the space below your name.

Name																

Getting Ahead in a Just-Gettin'-By World
Post-Workbook Participant Evaluation and Stages-of-Change Assessment

Facilitator:_____

Co-Facilitators:_____

ATTITUDE TOWARD THE FACILITATOR(S)

1.　　Had a helpful approach and style

Strongly disagree .... 1....2....3....4....5....6....7 Strongly agree

2.　　Provided a high-quality experience

Strongly disagree .... 1....2....3....4....5....6....7 Strongly agree

3.　　Treated people with respect

Strongly disagree .... 1....2....3....4....5....6....7 Strongly agree

ATTITUDE TOWARD THE WORKBOOK

4.　　Did not change my thinking.... 1....2....3....4....5....6....7 Did change my thinking

5.　　Not useful …......…..............1....2....3....4....5....6....7 Very useful

6.　　Not believable ……………….1....2....3....4....5....6....7 Very believable

USE OF INFORMATION

7.　　How likely is it that you will use the plans you made in your decision making?
　　　Unlikely ....1....2....3 Likely

8.　　Where are you in the stages of change? (Circle one and explain your answer.)

　　　Pre-Contemplation Contemplation Preparation Action Maintenance

9.　　What was most helpful thing about the workbook experience?

10.　　What was least helpful?

Comments:

Poverty Research Continuum
Causes and Cures of Poverty

Notes to the reader:

1. This table is available to people who have been through a Bridges workshop. It is a work in progress, a way of chunking information to better understand economic issues. It is the intellectual property of Philip DeVol and should not be used without permission.

2. This presentation of the research is intended to support the study of economics issues through the analytic category of economic class provided by Ruby Payne, Terie Dreussi Smith, and Philip DeVol (aha! Process, Inc.).

3. In her book *Poverty Knowledge: Social Science Policy and the Poor in Twentieth-Century U.S. History,* Alice O'Connor describes how political/economic forces use and misuse research to form policy. Ruby Payne's mental model of economic class provides a means for describing, analyzing, and predicting the behavior of each class as it pertains to poverty issues.

4. There are those who do the research and those who analyze it. I've put them (and some Websites) into the four categories knowing that many on the list do research that is more eclectic than their placement in the columns suggests. Michael Harrington, for example, appears in both the first and fourth columns because he described a culture of poverty but prescribed structural changes.

5. It seems clear that we won't end poverty unless we have a range or continuum of strategies at least as broad as the causes of poverty. In other words, within the four categories found in the following five pages, there is valid research that suggests the usefulness of many strategies. The list of strategies is not meant to be exhaustive; rather, it is merely an example of what may fall in each category.

6. For related readings, consult the bibliography that was provided at the workshop.

Finally, please send your comments, questions, and suggestions to me at the e-mail address below.

Philip E. DeVol: devol@bright.net

Poverty Research Continuum

CAUSES	Pathology of the Poor	Absence of Human and Social Capital	Colonial Exploitation	Political/ Economic Structures
RESEARCH TOPICS	Dependence on welfare Bad behavior of individuals Individual morality Bad behavior of groups Single parenthood Intergenerational character traits Bad mothers, mother-centered, matriarchal structures Values held by poor, lack of work ethic, commitment to achievement Breakup of families Addiction, mental illness, domestic violence	Lack of employment Lack of education Inadequate skill sets Decline in neighborhoods Big government Decline in social morality Urbanization Suburbanization of manufacturing "White flight" Inelastic cities: inadequate regional planning Immigration Failure of social services Absence of knowledge, worker skills, intellectual capital Social capital Lack of career ladder between knowledge and service sectors Speed of economic transformation at local level	Minimum wage vs. living wage Temporary jobs Less than 30 hours Lack of benefits Disposable employees Debt bondage Global outsourcing Payday lenders Lease/purchase Redlining Drug trade Exploitation for markets Exploitation of resources and raw materials	Policies that result in economic and social disparity Undue influence of corporations on legislation Tax structure that shifted tax burden to middle class, away from wealthy and corporations Decline in wages for bottom 90% Decline of unions De-industrialization Management/labor "bargain" CEO-to-line-worker salary ratio Profit/financial-centered form of globalization

www.ahaprocess.com

Poverty Research Continuum (continued)

CAUSES	Pathology of the Poor	Absence of Human and Social Capital	Colonial Exploitation	Political/ Economic Structures
ASSUMPTIONS	By studying the poor, we will learn what changes individuals must make in order to climb out of poverty. The poor are somehow lacking, either by their own bad choices or by circumstances. They should become "like us." Poverty is a sustainable condition.	By studying human and social capital, we will learn how to work within the larger political/economic structure to create conditions that foster prosperity. Faith that the market and market corrections will create most of the conditions necessary for general prosperity Acceptance of a 4 to 5% unemployment rate as an acceptable feature of the economy	By studying colonial and imperialist behavior, we can learn how to create just and equitable economic structures. Dominant groups discount the legitimacy of this category and look to the future. Dominated people (Appalachian, African Americans, Native Americans, former colonies) remember the past and may seek redress.	Studying the poor is not the same thing as studying poverty. Race, class, and gender are categories for analysis, not just demographics.
WHAT'S SAID	Don't blame the system; change the individual. Don't upset the system.	Don't blame the political/economic system; change the individual and the community system.	Upset the system and make it fair.	Don't blame the individual. Change the political/economic structure. Fight poverty instead of reforming welfare.

Poverty Research Continuum (continued)

CAUSES	Pathology of the Poor	Absence of Human and Social Capital	Colonial Exploitation	Political/ Economic Structures
SAMPLE FACTS	Number of words heard by age 3 by children in welfare, working class, and professional homes: 10 million, 20 million, and 30 million words, respectively. Prohibitions-to-encouragements ratio in responses to children in welfare, working class, and professional homes: 2:1, 1:2, 1:5, respectively. Average vocabulary of children at age 3 years in professional homes is 1,200 words. For adults in welfare homes it is 900 words used commonly in conversation (Hart/Risley). In 1960, for every 100 African-American single mothers there were 413 married couples; in 1995 for every 100 single mothers there were 63 married couples. Whites: 100 to 1,539 in 1960 and 100 to 422 in 1995 (Rusk).	"… [A]lmost 30 percent of the workforce toils for $8 an hour or less, as the Washington-based Economic Policy Institute reported in 1998 …" Ehrenreich). National Coalition for the Homeless, 1997: Nearly one-fifth of all homeless people in 29 cities are employed in full- or part-time jobs (Ehrenreich).	Developing countries send developed countries 10 times as much money through unequal trade and financial relations as they receive through foreign aid (United Nations). Eighty-four percent of the world's children are raised in poverty on income of less than $2 a day (Galeano). The United States represents 5% of the world's population— and uses 50% of the world's resources. Racism	"According to the National Coalition for the Homeless, in 1998 … it took, on average nationwide, an hourly wage of $8.89 to afford a one-bedroom apartment; the Preamble Center for Public Policy was estimating that the odds against a typical welfare recipient's landing a job at such a 'living wage' were about 97 to 1" (Ehrenreich). Economic disparity— top 10% getting richer, bottom 90% getting poorer—has been a growing trend since the 1970s (Brouwer). Tax shift from corporations to individuals: The 1940s corporations paid 33%, individuals 44%. The 1990s corporations paid 14%, individuals 73% (Brouwer).

Poverty Research Continuum (continued)

CAUSES	Pathology of the Poor	Absence of Human and Social Capital	Colonial Exploitation	Political/Economic Structures
SOURCES, RESEARCH INSTITUTES, ANALYSTS, WEBSITES	Michael Harrington, Betty Hart and Todd Risley, Oscar Lewis, Daniel Patrick Moynihan, Charles Murray, Jack Pransky American Enterprise Institute Brookings Institution Bureau of Applied Research, Columbia University Council for Urban Affairs Department of Social Relations, Harvard University Ford Foundation Heritage Foundation Institute for Social Research, University of Michigan Manhattan Institute University of Chicago www.financeproject.org www.heritage.org	David Brooks, Robert Lampman, John McKnight, Daniel Patrick Moynihan, Gunnar Myrdal, Robert Putnam, David Rusk, William Wilson American Council on Education Bureau of Applied Research, Columbia University Department of Social Relations, Harvard University Ford Foundation Institute for Social Research, University of Michigan University of Chicago University of Wisconsin, IRP Urban Institute www.childwelfare.com www.clasp.org www.cpmcnet.columbia.edu/dept/nccp/index.html www.mdrc.org www.urban.org www.welfareinfo.org www.wmadcampaign.org	Saul Alinksy, Kenneth Clark, Eduardo Galeano, Jim Goad, Margaret Hagood, Charles S. Johnson, Harvey Wasserman Economic Policy Institute of National Emergency Council www.northwestern.edu	Steve Brouwer, David Caplovitz, Osha Davidson, Hernando De Soto, Robert Frank, B. Franklin Frazier, Paulo Freire, John Kenneth Galbraith, Herbert Gans, Graham Hancock, Michael Harrington, Bell Hoods, Marjorie Kelly, Christopher Lasch, Charles Lewis, Robert Putnam, Robert Sapolsky, Muhammad Yunus Center for Budget and Policy Priorities Urban Institute www.acorn.org www.bettercommunities.org www.bread.org www.fair.org www.nlihc.org www.ufenet.org

Poverty Research Continuum (continued)

CAUSES	Pathology of the Poor	Absence of Human and Social Capital	Colonial Exploitation	Political/Economic Structures
STRATEGIES	Hold individual accountable and use sanctions if necessary. Target individuals. Work first. Self-sufficiency Enhance language experience. Psychology of mind Treatment interventions Resiliency Work ethic Mentors Literacy Asset development Abstinence education Marriage promotion Caseload reductions	Hold individual and social service systems accountable. Use sanctions if necessary. Full employment, growth in labor market Education Skill development Anti-poverty programs for childcare, child support, healthcare, housing EITC (earned income tax credit) Regional planning Community action programs Head Start Workforce Investment Act Continuous growth One-stop centers	Hold the colonialists (white, northern elite) accountable. Community-based development Political organizing to win control over economic and political institutions	Hold political/ economic power structure accountable. Use economic disparity trends as a measure. Interdisciplinary approach to macroeconomic planning and policies Whole-system planning Enhance living standards. Redistribution of wealth in other direction Access to capital and ownership

MENTAL MODEL FOR CREATING INDIVIDUAL
&
COMMUNITY PROSPERITY

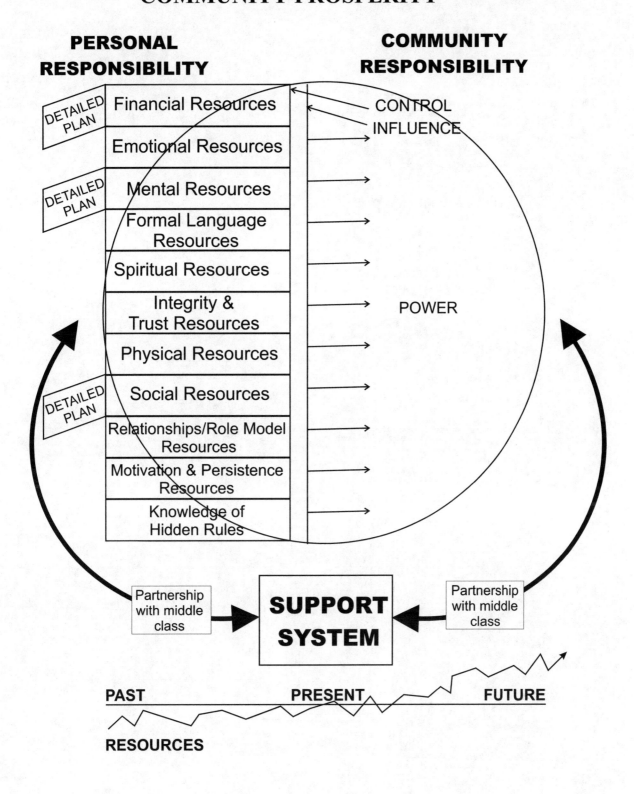

Activity 4: Income Quintiles

Trainer's Goals: a. To illustrate the information contained in the charts: "Income Growth 1979-2001" and "1947-1979"

This activity compares income distribution in two recent periods of economic growth in the U.S. To demonstrate the growth and decline of incomes in these two periods, five volunteer participants are asked to come up and stand in the front of the room. [For this activity to work well, the volunteers will need plenty of space to move forward and some space to move back.] It is important that the group focus on the top one to five percent of the population — the greatest beneficiaries of the growing divide. It is also important that everyone gets a chance to see where they fit, in terms of income distribution. Most folks think they are "middle income" and it is often a revelation to learn otherwise. We demonstrate the 1979-2001 time period before the 1947-1979 period because our experience has shown the activity to be more memorable that way. It also gets folks thinking about government programs that generally supported greater economic equality in the 1950s and 1960s (e.g., the GI Bill, appropriations for higher education, housing, and infrastructure projects, more favorable law inforcement, etc.).

Props: It is helpful to make 8.5" x 11" placards for each volunteer participant to hold, identifying the quintiles and showing the income range.

Instructions: 1. We are going to look at the changes in *family* income during two recent periods of economic growth. First, let's talk a little about income. What are some examples of income? (wages, salary, savings account interest, social security check, rent from owning real estate, capital gains from selling investments, dividends from stocks, gifts, etc.) Now let's have five volunteers come to the front of the room. Please stand should to shoulder. [The trainer hands each volunteer a placard showing the income range — in pre-tax, year 2001 dollars — of the quintile they represent.]

2. Listen to this introduction to the concept of income quintiles. Economists often talk about the U.S. population in "quintiles" or "fifths" of the population. They imagine the entire population of the U.S. lined up in order, from the lowest income to the highest. They then divide that line into five equal parts. This activity looks at what happened to the incomes during two periods of economic growth: 1947-1979 and 1979-2001. Let's look at some of the folks who are in these quintiles. What sorts of occupations or economic situations would you imagine fall into each quintile? Remember, this is *family* income. (A family is two or more related individuals living together.)

3. The following demonstration may seem like the childhood game "Mother May I" (also known as "Giant Steps"). Each volunteer, representing a quintile or fifth of the U.S. population, will step forward or back according to whether their income gained or declined. Each step equals a ten percent change, so, for example, two steps forward would indicate an income gain of 20%.

4. Between 1979 and 2001 (Chart #5), here's what happened:

Quintile	Steps	Percent Change	Yearly Income Range (2001) (family income before tax)
Lowest	1/2 step forward	+3%	$0 - 24,000
Second	1 step forward	+11%	$24,000 - 41,127
Middle	1 1/2 steps forward	+17%	$41,127 - 62,500
Fourth	2 1/2 steps forward	+26%	$62,500 - 94,150
Highest	5 1/2 steps forward	+53%	$94,150 & higher

5. Watch what happens when we break that top quintile down even further and look at only the richest five percent of the population. Rather than tear off the arm of our highest quintile volunteer, let's have another volunteer from the audience represent the top five percent— people with incomes of $164,104 and up. From 1979 to 2001, the income of this group grew 81%. [From the spot where the top quintile is standing, the sixth volunteer takes three additional steps forward – eight steps in total from the starting line].

Quintile	Steps	Percent Change	Yearly Income Range (family income before tax)
Top 5%	3 additional steps forward	+81%	$164,104 and up

6. Watch this demonstration of what happened to the quintiles during the post war years: 1947-1979. We will start with the top four quintiles. How well (number of steps forward or back) do you think the bottom quintile fared. How about the top five percent. What strikes you about these two periods in history?

Quintile	Steps	Percent change
Lowest	12 Steps Forward	+116%
Second	10 Steps Forward	+100%
Middle	11 Steps Forward	+111%
Fourth	11.5 Steps Forward	+114%
Highest	10 Steps Forward	+99%
Top 5%	8.5 Steps Forward	+86%

7. What conclusions do you draw about family incomes? What questions do you have?

8. Listen to this review of *Chart #5 Real Family Income Growth from 1979 to 2001* and *Chart #6: Real Family Income Growth from 1947 to 1979*. What are your questions?

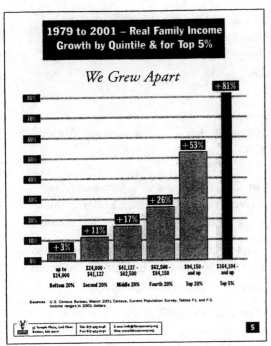

Chart #5: Family Income Growth, 1979–2001
Growing Apart

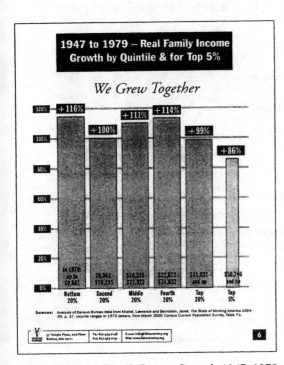

Chart #6: Family Income Growth, 1947–1979
Growing Together

Talking Points

♦ From 1979-2001, there was much growth in income, but the distribution of that growth was very uneven. Although the top 20% as a whole did well, the ones who really made out were the top 5%.

♦ Why this skew of income from 1979 - 2001?

- At the top, the biggest income growth source was income from assets (rental income, earnings from stocks, bonds and other investments, capital gains from sales of property and investments). Since asset ownership is heavily concentrated in the wealthiest 20%, it is not surprising that that's where the gains went.

- There was explosive growth in CEO salaries.

- At the bottom, the real value of the minimum wage was allowed to fall during the 1980s.

- A weakened labor movement was less able to prop up the wages of workers at the bottom of the scale.

♦ From 1947 to 1979, incomes for each quintile as a whole — from top to bottom — basically doubled. In fact, the greatest increase was experienced by the bottom 20%. And the smallest increase was experienced by the top 5%. In other words, the divide between top and bottom in America actually narrowed slightly during this period.

♦ However, while the rate of income growth during this period was generally the same for everyone within each quintile — the significant gap between the incomes of African Americans and white Americans remained wide (see Chart #7).

♦ The purpose of Chart #6 is not to glorify the 1950s but to point out that we achieved greater income equity across the quintiles. Also, the chart reflects the positive impact of social programs from the 1950s through the 1970s.

♦ The period from 1947 to 1979 demonstrates that the great disparity in the distribution of income growth, as happened from 1979 to 2001, is not inevitable. Rather, it is, in part, the result of deliberate government policies.

♦ The goal of the government during the early post-war period was to build a middle class. Programs such as the GI Bill — which allowed hundreds of thousands of returned veterans to go to college and purchase homes — were funded by relatively high taxes on the wealthy (the top tax rate was 91%). It is important to acknowledge that these programs disproportionally favored white men. For example, the VA and FHA loan programs for housing, both of which utilized racially-restrictive underwriting criteria, assured that hardly any of the $120 billion in housing equity loaned from the late 1940s to the early 1960s would go to families of color. These loans helped finance over half of all suburban housing construction in the country during this period, less than two percent of which ended up being lived in by people of color.

♦ The goal of the government during the 1980s and 1990s, however, was to let the rich accumulate great capital in the belief that it would trickle down.

Activity 6: The CEO Pay Gap

Trainers Goals: a. Dramatize the widening gap between the highest and the average paid workers in the U.S.

                   b. Explore why the wage gap in the U.S. is wider than in other nations.

This activity is a role play that illustrates the ratio between those who are paid the most — Chief Executive Officers (CEOs) and average workers. Six volunteers, each carrying an identifying sign, will role play CEOs and average workers from three different countries. The volunteers representing CEOs will move across the room in proportion to the difference between their compensation and their workers' pay.

Props for this learning activity:

- Placards that say: "Japanese Average Worker"   "German Average Worker"   "U.S. Average Worker"

                                 "Japanese CEO"   "German CEO"   "U.S. CEO"

Instructions: 1. Let's have six volunteers who will represent workers or CEOs from the U.S., Japan, and Germany line up in two columns facing the audience. One column represents the CEOs and the other column are average workers.* Please hold a sign identifying who you are so all can see.

             The U.S., Japanese, and German CEOs will move sideways step by step with each step equal to a five times ratio (therefore, if an average worker was paid $20,000 and the highest paid executive receives ten times that amount — $200,000 — then they would be two steps apart).

             The income ratio between the German CEO and the German worker is about 13 to one. The German CEO takes two and a half sideways steps. Next, the Japanese CEO — a little less than the German CEO (11 to one): two sideways steps. In the U.S. the ratio is 34 to one: seven steps. (See Chart 12: The Wage Gap Around the World.)

       *   These comparisons are for medium-size manufacturing firms surveyed by the Towers Perrin consulting firm in 2000.

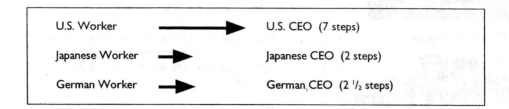

      2. Now, if we look at the 365 largest U.S. firms as reported in the Annual Executive Pay report by *Business Week*, in 1980 the ratio of CEO pay to the average worker was 42 to one (8 steps apart). In 2000, the ratio was 531 to one (106 steps apart).

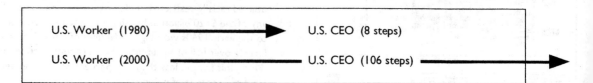

      3. What strikes you about the income ratio comparison? How would you explain the difference in income ratio between the U.S. and Germany and Japan? We will share some examples.

Talking Points

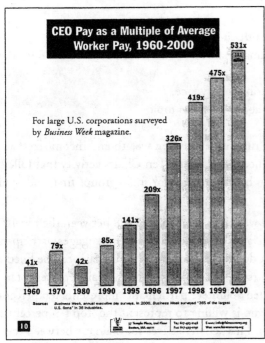

Chart #10: CEO Pay as a Multiple of Worker Pay

◆ 531 to one is the average wage ratio at 365 of the largest corporations, according to the 2000 Annual Executive Pay Survey of *Business Week*. Many large firms in the U.S. have even larger ratios. For example, the Disney Company's CEO, Michael Eisner, makes over 10,000 times his lowest paid worker (Minnie Mouse?) — a gap of 2,000 steps.

◆ CEO over-compensation hurts average Americans. It transfers wealth upward from employees and shareholders to already affluent top executives.

◆ Organizational management consultants, such as Peter Drucker, believe that corporations must flatten out their structures — which exist primarily to justify excessive salary differentials. He speaks specifically of establishing a wage ratio between top and bottom.

◆ In recent years, shareholder activists have begun to draw attention to the issue of the huge gaps between CEO and worker pay by demanding that the corporations set wage ratios. Contact UFE for more information about shareholder campaigns for pay equity.

Top Ten CEOs in 2000 (total compensation)

1. John Reed, Citigroup ($293 million)
2. Sanford Weill, Citigroup ($225 million)
3. Gerald Levin, AOL Time Warner ($164 million)
4. John Chambers, Cisco Systems ($157 million)
5. Henry Silverman, Cendant ($137 million)
6. L. Dennis Kozlowski, Tyco International ($125 million)
7. Jack Welch, General Electric ($123 million)
8. David Peterschmidt, Inktomi ($108 million)
9. Kevin Kalkhoven, Compuware ($107 million)
10. David Wetherell, CMGI ($104 million)

Talking Points

◆ Sanford Weill, CEO of Citigroup earned $225 million in 2000. That means he made $4,327,000 a week; $721,150 a day; $72,115 an hour. He earned 233 times the minimum hourly wage every minute! His compensation is about equivalent to 7,500 well-paid bank teller's salaries. Because of the cap on wages that are subject to the Social Security tax, Weill was done paying into Social Security at 11:00 a.m. on January 2nd, after his second hour of work. Most of us saw money taken out of every one of our paychecks.

◆ Some CEOs win big even when their company loses. Coca-Cola CEO Douglas Ivester resigned after a two-year tenure that produced a –7.3% return for shareholders, layoffs of thousands of workers and a lawsuit alleging the company discriminated against Black employees. For that, he walked away with stock options and other perks worth at least $120 million.

Chart #11: Business Week Cover: Executive Pay

◆ Bank America's CEO David Coulter made over $3.5 million in salary and bonuses in 1996 despite the fact that he laid off 3,700 workers. His salary breaks down to a little over $68,000 a week. The average entry level teller at Bank America who starts off at $7.50 an hour would have to work for 227 years to earn Coulter's yearly paycheck.

Activity 7: The Ten Chairs

Trainers Goals: a. To define and compare the concepts of "wealth" and "income."
 b. To dramatize wealth inequality and the dramatic shift in wealth from 1979 to 1998 for the top one percent.
 c. To demonstrate the disparity of wealth distribution by race.
 d. To use humor and have fun while learning about a serious topic.

The first part of this activity (see Instruction 1) establishes the difference between wealth and income so that participants will have a solid frame of reference as they experience the dramatic Ten Chairs activity that follows. With a lot of time, the discussion about wealth and income can happen in pairs or small groups first, and then a sample of responses can be shared.

The Ten Chairs activity portrays the distribution of household wealth in the U.S. in 1998 between the top 10% and everyone else, compares the distribution of wealth for the top 1% in 1976 and in 1998, and engages participants in dialogue about wealth inequality. It works best with chairs that do not have armrests. The chairs can be lined up across the front of the room facing the participants, prior to the start of the activity. Each chair represents ten percent of all the private wealth in the United States. Each of ten volunteer participants represents ten percent of the population of the U.S. It is helpful to identify one person who is willing to represent the "top ten percent" who may have a sense of humor or theatrical qualities (i.e., a "ham"). This activity strives for dialogue between the trainer and the volunteers in their roles as well as dialogue and reflection among all the participants. Remember to encourage a round of applause for all the volunteers at the end of this activity.

Instructions: 1. Listen to this standard (economist's) definition of wealth [see the first Q & A in the box below]. Name examples of assets that low-income, middle-income, and upper-income people might have [The trainer can note that there are other ways to view wealth, and participants can be asked to share alternative definitions, e.g., "a person can be considered rich in education, experience, influence, children, etc."]

What is Wealth?

Question: How is wealth different from income? What is wealth?

Answers: Wealth is private assets minus liabilities (debt). Simply put, wealth is **what you own** minus **what you owe.** Income is your paycheck or government benefit check or dividend check, or your profit from selling an investment. Wealth is what you have in the bank and the property you own.

Question: Is it possible to have negative wealth?

Answer: Yes. Nineteen percent of the population currently have no assets or they have negative assets: they owe more than they own.

Question: What are examples of assets that lower-income people might have?

Answer: Cash (savings or checking account), furniture, a car.

Question: What are examples of assets owned by middle-income people?

Answer: Cash (savings or checking account), equity in a house, a small business, a little bit of stock and/or a retirement fund.

Question: What are examples of assets owned by the top one percent?

Answer: Additional houses, real estate, large stock and bond holdings, businesses, paintings and other collectibles.

---

2. Let's have ten volunteers stand in front of one of the chairs. We need one person who is willing to be the "top ten percent." [Remember to try and select a person who is a bit of a ham.] Each person represents one-tenth of the US population and each chair represents one-tenth of all the private material wealth in the United States. If wealth were evenly distributed this is what it would look like — one person, one chair. [One variation is to have each person sit in a chair while the trainer makes the point that this picture of equal wealth distribution has never existed. When folks have to give up their chairs it ups the emotional punch of the activity.]

3. Currently (the most up-to-date data we have is for 1998), the top 10% owns 71% of all private wealth. The volunteer representing the top 10% takes over seven chairs "evicting" the current occupants and making her/himself comfortable on their expanded share of the wealth pie. The rest of the volunteers (representing 90% of the U.S. population) must share three chairs (or about 30% of the wealth pie). [*This may require some shepherding and encouragement. Groups less familiar with one another will cluster sitting and standing around the chairs.*]

4. Even within the top 10% there is great disparity — a disparity that has increased dramatically over the last 22 years. In 1976 the share of the top 1% was 22% (about 2 chairs). But by 1998, their share had nearly doubled to 38% of all wealth (about 4 chairs)! That's more chairs than the bottom 90% have combined! [To illustrate this, the trainer can let the arm of the volunteer representing the top 10% represent the wealthiest 1% of the households or you can use a top hat or other item of ostentatious wealth.

5. Notice the circumstances you are in and your own feelings about this. How are you feeling at the top? How about in the bottom 90%? If you were going to push someone off the chairs to make room who would it be? Why? What conclusions do you draw about the focus of public policy discussions — looking up the chairs (at the top one percent) or looking down the chairs at the disadvantaged? What questions do you have? [Often folks direct their anger at the person representing the top 10%. Yet in reality this group remains largely invisible to the rest while wedges based on race, gender, sexual orientation, age, and class are driven between folks and we all battle each other for more space on the few remaining chairs.]

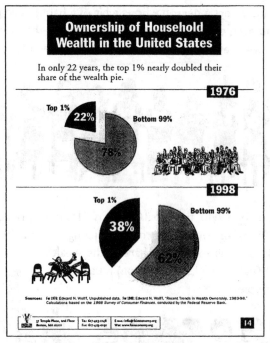

Chart #14: Ownership of Household Wealth in the U.S.

Talking Points

♦ Wealth is private assets minus liabilities (debt). Simply put, it is what you own minus what you owe.

♦ The shift in wealth (from 1976 to 1998) is an alarming one in so short a time frame (about 20 years). During this time period, the share of the wealth pie of the top one percent nearly doubled.

♦ Even though the "pie" grew from 1976 to 1998, wealth is now more concentrated in the U.S. than at any time since the 1920s.

♦ The share of private wealth owned by the top one percent now is more than the bottom 90% of the population combined. In fact, one man, Bill Gates, all by himself, has as much wealth as the bottom 40% of all households in the U.S.

♦ What does this distribution mean for the lives of most people? Declining net worth (growing personal indebtedness); less home ownership; no stake in a pension fund.

♦ In 1982, the wealthiest 400 individuals in the Forbes 400 owned $92 billion. By 2000, their wealth increased to over $1.2 trillion.

♦ Too much wealth in too few hands fuels speculation from the top, de-stabilizing the jobs and security of many people. Besides, there are only so many race horses, works of art, or face lifts any one person can have. More money in more people's hands would be a better fuel for the economy. As economist Randy Albelda put it: "Mink coats don't trickle down."

♦ The shift in the ownership of income and wealth — and the changing nature of work — will likely hit the next generation particularly hard. Many young people who grew up in middle class families may never have a standard of living approaching their parents — and therefore will increasingly be dependent on their parent's savings (equity) to help them build any security. Lower income youth face the prospect of a lifetime of economic insecurity.

♦ Wealth begets wealth. The impact of compounding interest multiplies wealth for asset holders.

♦ According to the Federal Reserve's 2001 Survey of Consumer Finances, the wealth gap between the top ten percent and the 20 percent of families with the lowest incomes jumped 70 percent from 1998 through 2001. For the same period, median net worth (assets minus debt) of families of color fell 4.5% and the gap between these families and white families grew by 21%.

Where Do We Go from Here? How Do Communities Develop Intellectual Capital and Sustainability?

by Ruby K. Payne, Ph.D.

A key discussion in the United States in the new millennium centers on community. Urban areas have not had a good model for community. Rural areas are losing population and the sense of community they have always had. In fact, the only community that many rural areas have anymore is the local school district. As the student count shrinks and conversations about consolidation begin, many communities vigorously resist that effort because intuitively they understand the need for community.

For the purposes of this article, the definition of community will be the one used by Carl Taylor and Daniel Taylor-Ide in the book *Just and Lasting Change: When Communities Own Their Futures*. They write: "Community, as we use the term, is any group that has something in common and the potential for acting together" (page 19).

Taylor and Taylor-Ide have been involved with community development for many years around the world. "The key to building better lives," they state, "is not technical breakthroughs but changing behavior at the community level … in ways that fit local circumstances … Playing an essential role in these processes are the formation and maintenance of a genuine three-way partnership among people in the community, experts from the outside, and government officials" (pages 17–18).

Community development is becoming more imperative because of the relationship between the intellectual capital in the community and its economic well-being.

What is intellectual capital?

Thomas Stewart, in his book *Intellectual Capital: The New Wealth of Organizations,* defines it as the "intangible assets—the talents of its people, the efficacy of its management systems, the character of its relationships to its customers …" It is the ability to take existing information and turn it into useful knowledge and tools.

Intellectual capital has become the economic currency of the 21st century. In the 1900s the economic currency was industry-based. In the 1800s it was agriculture-based. One of the issues for many communities is the loss of jobs related to industry and agriculture. Wealth creation is now linked to intellectual capital.

What is the relationship between economic well-being and the development of capital?

Right now in the world and in the United States there is a direct correlation between the level of educational attainment in a community or country and its economic wealth. In the book *As the Future Catches You*, Juan Enriquez gives the following statistic: In 1980 the differential between the richest and poorest country in the world was 5:1 as measured by GNP. In 2001 the differential between the richest and the poorest country in the world was 390:1 as measured by gross national product. GNP is directly linked to the level of educational attainment. So growth is not incremental; it is exponential.

For the future well-being of communities, it becomes necessary to begin the serious and deliberate development of intellectual capital. This is easier said than done.

How do communities develop intellectual capital? How do you translate between the poor and the policy makers/power brokers?

Systems tend to operate out of default and are amoral. Systems are only as moral as the people who are in them. One of the big issues is how different economic groups translate the issues. For a group to work together, there must be a shared understanding and vocabulary. What is a huge issue to an individual in poverty often doesn't translate as an issue in wealth. The policymakers/power brokers tend to be at the wealth level, while the bureaucrats are at the middle-class level. In the book *Seeing Systems*, Barry Oshry talks about the difficulty the three levels have in communicating with each other.

The chart identifies how issues are addressed at different economic levels.

POVERTY	MIDDLE CLASS	WEALTH
Having a job Hourly wages	Appropriate, challenging job Salary and benefits	Maintenance and growth of assets Quality and quantity of workforce
Safety of schools	Quality of schools	K–12 higher education continuum Technical innovation Intermediate colleges and trade schools
A place to rent/live Affordable housing	Property values Quality of schools Quality of neighborhood	Corporate investment potential Infrastructure to support development

www.ahaprocess.com

Welfare benefits	Taxes	Balance of trade
		Percentage of taxes
		Tort liability
		Corporate contributions
		Percentage of government indebtedness
Fairness of law enforcement	Safety	Risk management
Gangs	Crime rates	Bond ratings
		Insurance ratings
Access to emergency rooms	Cost of medical insurance	Cost/predicted costs of medical benefits
	Quality and expertise of medical profession	Workers' compensation
Public transportation	Network of freeways	Systems of transportation (railway, bus, air, etc.)
	Traffic congestion	
	Time commuting	Maintenance of the infrastructure
Have enough food	Access to quality restaurants	Access to high-quality restaurants
	Variety/quality of food available	Amenities for clients
		Availability of fresh food

As you can see, the same issue is approached and viewed very differently, depending on the economic level of the individual.

<u>What would be the advantage to a community to translate between and among levels for a shared understanding</u>?

With shared understandings, one can develop community, create economic well-being, and develop sustainability.

<u>What is sustainability</u>?

Many people believe that the first major revolution in the world was the agricultural revolution when people were not moving but "stayed put" and had time to develop crafts and skills—and devote time to learning. Many also believe that the second major revolution was the industrial revolution when tools were used to spur development. Finally, the third major revolution may well be the development of sustainability. In other words, how do we use our resources, yet have enough available for the next generation? How do we live in our environment, yet maintain it for our children?

The following index lists major areas of sustainability.

SUSTAINABLE DEVELOPMENT INDEX (SDI)

1. Human rights, freedom, quality	A. Politics and human rights
	B. Equality
2. Demographic development and life expectancy	C. Demographic development
	D. Life expectancy, mortality
3. State of health and healthcare	E. Healthcare
	F. Disease and nutrition
4. Education	G. Education
	H. Technologies and information sharing
5. Economic development and foreign indebtedness	I. Economy
	J. Indebtedness
6. Resource consumption, eco-efficiency	K. Economy—genuine savings
	L. Economy—resource consumption
7. Environmental quality, environmental pollution	M. Environment—natural resources, land use
	N. Environment—urban and rural problems

This is the Sustainable Development Index (SDI) developed in 2000–01 by the Central European Node of the Millennium Project through the American Council for the United Nations University. In 1987 the World Commission on Environment and Development defined sustainability as a concept. In 1992 a total of 178 states agreed at the United Nations Conference of Environment and Development to include this concept in official development measures. Consensus appears to be emerging that sustainable development may well be "the third global revolution," following the agricultural and industrial revolutions (Mederly, Novacek, Topercer, pages 5, 8).

It is from the first four elements (above left) that intellectual capital is developed. Those four are foundational to the development of all others.

Why must equity precede sustainability?

One of the most interesting dynamics in communities is the impact of critical mass and equity on change. Thomas Sowell, a historical and international demographer, states that if a community allows any group to be disenfranchised for any reason (religion, race, class, etc.), the whole community becomes economically poorer. What happens is as follows:

10%	20%	30%	40%	50%	60%	70%	80%	90%	(top 10%)

Let's use poverty as an example. When 10% of a community is poor, most members of the community will say they have no poverty. When the number climbs to 20%, most will say there is very little poverty. When the number climbs to 30%, the comment will be that there are a few individuals in poverty in the community. But when it hits 35 to 40%, the community becomes alarmed. (Thirty-five to 40% is typically the point of critical mass. Critical mass is when enough people are involved that the issue/behavior gets above the radar screen and the community notices.) Comments are made that, all of a sudden, all these poor people came!

At that point in time, the top 10% of the community, which has most of the money and resources, will typically pass laws and ordinances to control the 40%. In the United States now the top 10% of households (as measured by income) pays 70% of all federal taxes. The bottom 50% of households pay 4% of federal taxes. By the time the poor population reaches 60 to 70% of the total community population, the top 10% of households will move out, leaving the community with very few resources. The community is no longer sustainable.

What process can communities use to develop both intellectual capital and sustainability?

To foster community involvement, it's important to use processes that are relatively simple and involve a large number of people, so that critical mass can be achieved. This process must be at least a 20- to 25-year plan, because it takes that long to get critical mass. As Paul Saffo, director of the Institute for the Future, states, "It takes 20 years to become an overnight success" (*BusinessWeek,* August 25, 2003).

It is my recommendation that communities secure endowments. What the endowment does is ensure that for 25 years the ensuing process is followed, data are collected, and three groups are always involved: people in the community, outside experts, and government officials.

The process I recommend takes a minimum of 20 years and follows these steps:

Step 1:

A community group gets together. The members of the group identify what their ideal community would be like 20 years hence. They identify six or seven issues (using the sustainability index as a guide) that would most enhance their community.

Step 2:

The group identifies the key markers for each issue that would indicate progress toward that ideal.

Step 3:

The group identifies the current status of those indicators by gathering "real" community data.

Step 4:

The group works backward and identifies what the marker would look like 18 years from the goal, 16 years from the goal, etc. Measurements for the markers are established.

Step 5:

The group goes to the larger community (including government officials) and asks all agencies, foundations, charities, churches, businesses, etc., which if any of the markers they are currently working on or would be willing to help address. The larger community agrees to gather data and report that data once a year.

Step 6:

The individuals overseeing the endowment gather the data, put it into a report and, once a year, gather all the larger community for a breakfast and report the data. The leadership persons make suggested recommendations for external expert assistance. The larger community recommits for another year to the larger goals and collection of data.

Step 6 is repeated every year.

It will take 10–12 years before much progress at all is seen. Then the progress will become noticeable. Within 20 years the progress will be dramatic.

Why use this process?

In the history of community development, one of four approaches tends to be used: blueprint, explosion, additive, or biological (Taylor and Taylor-Ide). The biological approach is one of tensegrity. "Tensegrity is the biological form of building," say the authors. "It works by balancing systems in flexible homeostasis rather than by building in a mechanical way that attaches its components rigidly" (page 58). According to Taylor and Taylor-Ide, tensegrity has these characteristics:
- It allows forms to move and reshape.
- It uses self-assembly in locally specific patterns.
- The whole is different from the member parts.
- It has information feedback.
- It has an efficient distribution and redistribution system.
- It brings accountability; when one part is irresponsible, the whole system is out of balance.

www.ahaprocess.com

<u>What can you do to get individuals from poverty involved in community issues?</u>

1. Understand the nature of systems. What appeals to the decision makers and power brokers doesn't have the same appeal in poverty and vice versa.
2. Work on real issues—issues that impact day-to-day life.
3. Approach the poor as problem solvers, not victims.
4. Teach the adult voice.
5. Teach question making.
6. Teach "backward" planning ("begin with the end in mind").
7. Start the process by building relationships of mutual respect, using videos, food, and entertainment; identify the power brokers in the poor community (corner grocers, hairdressers, barbers, ministers, etc.) and bring them into the process.
8. Pay them for their time (e.g., with inexpensive gift cards).
9. Let them bring their children.
10. Identify common tasks so that conversation can occur.
11. Provide constructive outlets for frustration and criticism.
12. Use mental models to help identify, with a minimum of emotion, the areas of needed change.
13. Gather real data.

<u>Why would a community consider such an endowed process?</u>

Quoting Taylor and Taylor-Ide, "For rich and poor alike, the expansion of trade, changes in the Earth's environment, and the unraveling of social systems make the future uncertain. Even wealthy societies are increasingly unable to care for their growing numbers of poor, alienated youth, forgotten elderly, marginalized mothers, hostile homeless, and exploited minorities … To achieve a more just and lasting future, we must continually update our definition of development. We can advance more confidently and effectively into that unknown territory be drawing lessons from past successes—and from past failures—and by tailoring solutions for each community to its specific hopes, capabilities, and resources" (page 30).

In short, community development—based on intellectual capital—is not a choice. Our sustainability, even survival, depends on it.

BRIDGES OUT OF POVERTY
COMMUNITY SUSTAINABILITY GRID

	RESEARCH AREAS			
ACTION AREAS	**BEHAVIORS OF INDIVIDUAL**	**HUMAN AND SOCIAL CAPITAL**	**EXPLOITATION**	**POLITICAL/ ECONOMIC STRUCTURES**
INDIVIDUAL ACTION				
ORGANIZATIONAL ACTION				
COMMUNITY ACTION				
POLICY CHANGE				

Appendix I

Model Fidelity Elements
for Conducting
Getting Ahead in a Just-Gettin'-By World

Prepared by Philip E. DeVol

Thanks to feedback from facilitators and sponsors who use *Getting Ahead,* we have learned what elements of our model are essential. In other words, we can now define our model. In order to adhere to our model, sponsors and facilitators are asked to attend to the following:

Role, Responsibilities, and Skills of the Facilitator:

1. <u>Problem solvers</u>: Our view (or mental model) of *Getting Ahead* participants must be based on the understanding that they are problem solvers in their daily lives and can be problem solvers at the community level. They are needed at the planning tables in our communities.

2. <u>Investigators</u>: *Getting Ahead* participants are most accurately described as "investigators." They investigate community life, as well as their personal circumstances in light of the new learning they're doing. Each module is another layer of that investigation. It isn't the facilitator's job to defend everything in the workbook; it's the facilitator's job to help the investigators dig into the material.

3. <u>Sequence and reinforcement</u>: The sequence has been worked out carefully so that investigators move from the safe to the challenging, the concrete to the abstract, and the small to the large. It allows for reinforcement of the difficult concepts and is not to be altered.

4. <u>Motivation for change</u>: Those who participate in the workgroup are not expected to be motivated for change at the outset. The process and the facilitator assist people to make their own arguments for change. It isn't necessary for the facilitator to make the arguments; in fact, the facilitator is advised not to make the arguments for change. Facilitators who adhere to this model and have the ability to assist another person's process of self-discovery are to be prized.

5. <u>Mental models</u>: The investigators are asked to end the workgroup with mental models of their own making that describe their process, hold the knowledge of their investigation, and guide their action.

6. <u>Self-assessment</u>: Developing a plan without doing an accurate self-assessment is meaningless. The quality of the plan stems from the quality of thinking that goes into the assessment; therefore, it's necessary to practice analyzing resources using the case studies found in *Bridges Out of Poverty*.

7. <u>Community assessment</u>: This assessment is equally important and is to arise out of the work of the group. Community organizations should not be brought in for "dog and pony shows."

8. <u>Personal and community plans</u>: The ultimate goal is to create plans for building resources on personal and community levels.

9. <u>Facilitator characteristics</u>: Select facilitators who have the knowledge, skills, and attitudes described in the "*Getting Ahead* Facilitator Qualities" (see Appendix J).

Sponsor Responsibilities:

10. <u>Attraction, not coercion</u>: Planners are often pushed for quick results and think that forcing people to attend a particular workshop will bring the desired outcome. We, on the other hand, think this learning experience will attract people through word of mouth. Sanctions for failing to attend are unnecessary, even counterproductive.

11. <u>Stipends</u>: Administrators are often driven to be cost-effective. This means doing more with less—in this case, less money. Choosing not to pay stipends appears on the surface to be an easy solution. But paying stipends makes the point that people in poverty have something to offer the decision-making process in our communities, that the results of the *Getting Ahead* investigation have value, and that the investigators are being paid for their work.

12. <u>Fifteen sessions</u>: Another way of doing more for less is to reduce the amount of time given to the work, i.e., to cut down on the number of sessions. Fifteen weeks is the minimum amount of time needed to cover the information.

13. <u>Closed group</u>: There are two reasons for running the workbook with the same set of investigators from beginning to end. Having new people join the group means that they will not experience the sequence of learning as it works best. Second, the *Getting Ahead* process is based on a growing sense of trust and shared experiences.

14. <u>Long-term support</u>: The responsibility for this element falls on the sponsors of the workgroup more than on the facilitator. They are to be champions for the *Getting Ahead* investigators, making a place for them to build resources according to their own plans—and engaging the community to assist them during their transition. The investigators themselves may have plans of their own regarding long-term support; the sponsors are to be prepared to assist them.

15. <u>Getting to the table</u>: If the investigators want to take part in community planning and decision-making, i.e., if they want to "get to the table," the sponsor and facilitator need to be prepared to assist and mentor them, as well as to prepare the community for their participation.

Getting Ahead **Facilitator Qualities**

Effective *Getting Ahead* facilitators will have the knowledge, skills, and attitude described below:

Knowledge

- A *Getting Ahead* facilitator will be familiar with *Bridges Out of Poverty* concepts as taught in a one-day workshop.
- These concepts include: Mental Model of Poverty, Research Realities, Key Points, Hidden Rules, Language, Family, and Resources.

Skills

- Has the ability to make connections with others, particularly people from poverty.
- Can translate from the formal register to the casual register.
- Can facilitate another person's self-discovery.
- Can be empathetic without being "taken in."
- Has the ability to work with a co-facilitator who was a previous workshop participant.
- Has the ability to work effectively as someone from the dominant culture.

Attitude

- Likes people from poverty; in this work it's more important that we like the members of the workgroup than that they like us.
- Is a survivor who doesn't carry the "baggage."
- Doesn't believe that he/she has all the answers, i.e., knows that the answers must come from the participants.
- Sees the best in those who can't always see it in themselves.
- Can laugh and have fun.
- Is non-judgmental.
- Is willing to adhere to the *Getting Ahead/Bridges* model.

BIBLIOGRAPHY

Getting Ahead Facilitator Training

Alexie, Sherman. (1993). *The Lone Ranger and Tonto Fistfight in Heaven.* New York, NY: HarperPerennial.

Andreas, Steve, & Faulkner, Charles. (Eds.). (1994). *NLP: The New Technology of Achievement.* New York, NY: Quill.

Bonilla-Silva, Eduardo. (2003). *Racism Without Racists: Color-Blind Racism and the Persistence of Racial Inequality in the United States.* Lanham, MD: Rowman & Littlefield Publishers.

Brouwer, Steve. (1998). *Sharing the Pie: A Citizen's Guide to Wealth and Power in America.* New York, NY: Henry Holt & Company.

Covey, Stephen R. (1989). *The Seven Habits of Highly Effective People: Powerful Lessons in Personal Change.* New York, NY: Fireside Book, Simon & Schuster.

DeNavas-Walt, Carmen, Proctor, Bernadette D., & Lee, Cheryl Hill. (2005). *Income, Poverty, and Health Insurance Coverage in the United States: 2004.* Washington, DC: U.S. Census Bureau, Current Population Reports, pp. 60–229, U.S. Government Printing Office.

Farson, Richard. (1997). *Management of the Absurd: Paradoxes in Leadership.* New York, NY: Touchstone.

Freedman, Jill, & Combs, Gene. (1996). *Narrative Therapy: The Social Construction of Preferred Realities.* New York, NY: W.W. Norton & Company.

Freire, Paulo. (1999). *Pedagogy of the Oppressed.* New York, NY: The Continuum Publishing Company.

Fussell, Paul. (1983). *Class: A Guide Through the American Status System.* New York, NY: Touchstone.

Galeano, Eduardo. (1998). *Upside Down: A Primer for the Looking-Glass World.* New York, NY: Metropolitan Books.

Gans, Herbert J. (1995). *The War Against the Poor.* New York, NY: Basic Books.

Gladwell, Malcolm. (2005). The moral-hazard myth: the bad idea behind our failed health-care system. *The New Yorker.* August 29.

Gladwell, Malcolm. (2000). *The Tipping Point: How Little Things Can Make a Big Difference.* Boston, MA: Little, Brown & Company.

Glasmeier, Amy K. (2006). *An Atlas of Poverty in America: One Nation, Pulling Apart, 1960–2003*. New York, NY: Routledge Taylor & Francis Group.

Goleman, Daniel. (1995). *Emotional Intelligence*. New York, NY: Bantam Books.

Harrison, Lawrence E., & Huntington, Samuel P. (Eds.). (2000). *Culture Matters: How Values Shape Human Progress*. New York, NY: Basic Books.

Hart, Betty, & Risley, Todd R. (1995). *Meaningful Differences in the Everyday Experience of Young American Children*. Baltimore, MD: Paul H. Brookes Publishing Co.

Henderson, Nan (1996). *Resiliency in Schools: Making It Happen for Students and Educators*. Thousand Oaks, CA: Corwin Press.

Kahn, Si, & Minnich, Elizabeth. (2005). *The Fox in the Henhouse: How Privatization Threatens Democracy*. San Francisco, CA: Berrett-Koehler Publishers.

Kelly, Marjorie. (2001). *The Divine Right of Capital: Dethroning the Corporate Aristocracy*. San Francisco, CA: Berrett-Koehler Publishers.

Kretzmann, John, & McKnight, John. (1993). *Building Communities from the Inside Out: A Path Toward Finding and Mobilizing a Community's Assets*. Chicago, IL: ACTA Publications.

Kusserow, Adrie. (2005). The workings of class: how understanding a subtle difference between social classes can promote equality in the classroom—and beyond. *Stanford Social Innovation Review*. Stanford, CA: Stanford Graduate School of Business. www.ssireview.com (accessed Spring 2006).

Lareau, Annette. (2003). *Unequal Childhoods: Class, Race, and Family Life*. Berkeley, CA: University of California Press.

Lind, Michael. (2004). Are we still a middle-class nation? *The Atlantic*. Volume 293. Number 1. January-February. pp. 120–128.

Lobovits, Dean, & Prowell, John. *Unexpected Journey: Invitations to Diversity*. www.narrativeapproaches.com (accessed Spring 2006).

Lui, Meizhu, Robles, Barbara, Leondar-Wright, Betsy, Brewer, Rose, & Adamson, Rebecca. (2006). *The Color of Wealth: The Story Behind the U.S. Racial Wealth Divide*. New York, NY: The New Press.

Mattaini, Mark A. (1993). *More Than a Thousand Words: Graphics for Clinical Practice*. Washington, DC: NASW Press.

McCarthy, Bernice. (2000). *About Learning: 4MAT in the Classroom*. Chicago, IL: About Learning.

McKnight, John. (1995). *The Careless Society: Community and Its Counterfeits*. New York, NY: Basic Books.

Miller, William R., & Rollnick, Stephen. (2002). *Motivational Interviewing: Preparing People for Change*, Second Edition. New York, NY: Guilford Press.

Miringoff, Marc, & Miringoff, Marque-Luisa. (1999). *The Social Health of the Nation: How America Is Really Doing*. New York, NY: Oxford University Press.

O'Connor, Alice. (2001). *Poverty Knowledge: Social Science, Social Policy, and the Poor in Twentieth-Century U.S. History*. Princeton, NJ: Princeton University Press.

Phillips, Kevin. (2002). *Wealth and Democracy: A Political History of the American Rich*. New York, NY: Broadway Books.

Pransky, Jack. (1998). *Modello: A Story of Hope for the Inner-City and Beyond*. Cabot, VT: NEHRI Publications.

Putnam, Robert D. (2000). *Bowling Alone: the Collapse and Revival of American Community*. New York, NY: Simon & Schuster.

Sapolsky, Robert M. (1998). *Why Zebras Don't Get Ulcers: An Updated Guide to Stress, Stress-Related Diseases, and Coping*. New York, NY: W.H. Freeman & Company.

Senge, Peter M. (1994). *The Fifth Discipline: The Art & Practice of the Learning Organization*. New York, NY: Doubleday-Currency.

Sered, Susan Starr, & Fernandopulle, Rushika. (2005). *Uninsured in America: Life and Death in the Land of Opportunity*. Berkeley, CA: University of California Press.

Sharron, Howard, & Coulter, Martha. (1996). *Changing Children's Minds: Feuerstein's Revolution in the Teaching of Intelligence*. Birmingham, England: Imaginative Minds.

Shipler, David K. (2004). *The Working Poor: Invisible in America*. New York, NY: Alfred A. Knopf.

Vella, Jane. (2002). *Learning to Listen, Learning to Teach: The Power of Dialogue in Educating Adults*. San Francisco, CA: Jossey-Bass.

Wheatley, Margaret J. (1992). *Leadership and the New Science: Learning About Organization from an Orderly Universe*. San Francisco, CA: Berrett-Koehler Publishers.

World Bank. (2005). *World Development Report 2006: Equity and Development*. New York, NY: Oxford University Press.

Prepared by Philip E. DeVol